G000039086

# ADVENTUROUS PUB WALKS
## IN
# LINCOLNSHIRE

**Roger Fox**

COUNTRYSIDE BOOKS
NEWBURY BERKSHIRE

First published 2004
© Roger Fox, 2004

All rights reserved. No reproduction
permitted without the prior permission
of the publisher:

COUNTRYSIDE BOOKS
3 Catherine Road
Newbury, Berkshire

To view our complete range of books,
please visit us at
www.countrysidebooks.co.uk

ISBN 1 85306 796 2

Photographs by the author
Designed by Peter Davies, Nautilus Design
Cover picture of Belchford supplied
by Malcolm Sales

Produced through MRM Associates Ltd., Reading
Typeset by Techniset Typesetters, Newton-le-Willows
Printed by J. W. Arrowsmith Ltd., Bristol

# CONTENTS

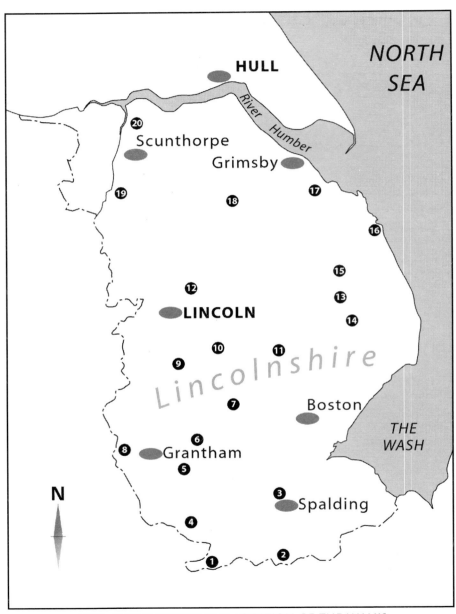

NORTH SEA

HULL

River Humber

⑳

Scunthorpe

Grimsby

⑲

⑱

⑰

⑯

⑮

⑬

⑫

**LINCOLN**

⑭

⑩

⑪

Lincolnshire

⑨

⑦

Boston

THE WASH

⑥

⑧ Grantham

⑤

N

❸

Spalding

❹

❷

❶

AREA MAP SHOWING THE LOCATION OF THE WALKS

# INTRODUCTION

If a gentle, level stroll to pass an hour or two is what you're looking for, you should put this book down now and move on to the next shelf. For the walks you will find here are walks with a difference. Chapter by chapter you will be taken deep into the heart of the exhilarating Lincolnshire countryside. These routes will unveil riches out of bounds to the motorist, cyclist and casual walker – you will discover the undiscovered. You may become so immersed in a landscape abounding in natural and historical treasures that the vexations of daily life will evaporate into the skies above you. A short stroll is always commendable, an invigorating and inexpensive way of making one feel good, but a long excursion such as you will find here adds a new dimension to your life. It transports you into a world far above the constraints of normal life, and is the perfect antidote for those feeling the need to escape for a few hours.

And nowhere can such solitude be enjoyed as in Lincolnshire. Can any other county offer such a diversity of walking possibilities? Here densely wooded valleys rise to chalky wolds summits, wide rivers cut through the vastness of the haunting fens, and huge skies full of ever-changing colours and cloud formations pass overhead. Her eastern boundary is a coastline divided into deserted sweeping sandy beaches, muddy estuaries rich in birdlife, lively seaside resorts like Skegness and Cleethorpes and, of course, major harbours at Boston and Grimsby, once the world's premier fishing port.

This whole county is crossed and re-crossed by a network of routes, ancient and not so ancient. Two Roman causeways – Ermine Street and the Fosseway – converge at Lincoln, whilst modern recreational routes such as the Viking Way, the Jurassic Way and the Macmillan Way link other parts of the area, and the glories of a bygone era of rail travel are witnessed by mile upon mile of disused track bed.

Buildings of great splendour and national importance are everywhere. Grimsthorpe Castle boasts the finest that Sir John Vanbrugh and Capability Brown could create, and the massive medieval brick keep of Tattershall Castle is nowhere surpassed. The behaviour of Grimsby's authorities in destroying the heritage of their own fishing industry may make Doctor Beeching seem like some benevolent old uncle, but the Dock Tower still remains a unique and breathtaking landmark, visible from far across the county. The minster crowning the limestone cliff in Lincoln is, of course, the jewel in the county's crown. But almost every settlement – down to the tiniest hamlet – can boast an intriguing church or a Georgian chapel. Lincolnshire was a 17th century stronghold of nonconformity and reminders abound, from the birthplace of John Wesley in Epworth to the sailing point of the Pilgrim Fathers on the Boston shoreline. White-capped windmill towers (England's tallest is at Moulton), peaceful grassy towpaths along once industrious canals, sites of deserted villages decimated by the Black Death and countless former World War II aviation sites that once earned Lincolnshire the epithet 'Bomber County' are also on offer. Lincolnshire is many things, but 'the most brute and beastly shire of the realm' as branded by Henry VIII? That it is not.

Lincolnshire does many things well, but providing delicious, traditional foodstuffs is probably what it does best, whether it be freshly smoked fish from Grimsby or herb-stuffed chine from Mareham-le-Fen. Lincolnshire sausages enjoy an unrivalled reputation, while tasty ice cream and tempting ales are produced throughout the region. And this tasty fare can be found in most of the inns at your mid-ramble halts. These hostelries are diverse and well spread out, and their reasons for inclusion are many. However, they all have some qualities in common. All offer first class meals at sensible prices, and well-kept ales – with an interesting guest beer or two thrown in. A warm welcome can be expected at every one, comfortable and interesting surroundings too. A note of caution, though – the quiet nature of the Lincolnshire countryside means that opening times can vary from those stated, especially in winter and on some weekdays. All telephone numbers are included, so please ring to confirm before you set off.

Unlike many guidebooks your walks do not begin at the featured inn, and you are urged to park considerately at the start of the route. In many cases this will be limited roadside parking. The nature of the walks also means that some navigational ability is required and, although the maps included in the text will give you some assistance around the circuit, aided by numbered indicators, the use of the corresponding Ordnance Survey map is strongly recommended. These maps not only simplify path-finding but also display a wealth of additional information to make your walk that much more rewarding. You will not need telling that warm and waterproof clothing and a good pair of walking boots should be treated as essential gear. All of the walks should be treated as full-day excursions, with a stop at the inn mid-way. Some can be easily curtailed if time demands, but I should steer you away from this option as a lot of the walks are designed to display their best features on the 'homeward' leg – you have, after all, enlisted for adventure.

So, if you long to combine your love of walking and of fine country inns with your yearning for adventure, take up the gauntlet and read on. Rise to the challenge and head for the remoteness of the Lincolnshire landscape, ever varied, ever changing. Come and search for the spirit of the land that so inspired Alfred Lord Tennyson, the land whose diversity of mood is fleetingly disclosed by Sir John Betjeman in *A Lincolnshire Church*:

'Greyly tremendous the thunder
Hung over the width of the wold
But here the green marsh was alight
In a huge cloud cavern of gold.'

Maybe then you will come to share my deep affection for Lincolnshire, this most remarkable and rewarding of counties. It is to the patience and imagination of my mother that I owe my love of the area in which I grew up, its history and heritage, its variety and its beauty. How fitting it would be if this book of hike and hostelry were to inspire her to once again roam the green lanes and pathways of Lincolnshire. She's also partial to a glass of Bateman's!

Happy walking!

Roger Fox

## PUBLISHER'S NOTE

We hope that you obtain considerable enjoyment from this book; great care has been taken in its preparation. Although at the time of publication all routes followed public rights of way or permitted paths, diversion orders can be made and permissions withdrawn.

We cannot, of course, be held responsible for such diversion orders and any inaccuracies in the text which result from these or any other changes to the routes nor any damage which might result from walkers trespassing on private property. We are anxious though that all details covering the walks are kept up to date and would therefore welcome information from readers which would be relevant to future editions.

The simple sketch maps that accompany the walks in this book are based on notes made by the author whilst checking out the routes on the ground. However, for the benefit of a proper map, we do recommend that you purchase the relevant Ordnance Survey sheet covering your walk. The Ordnance Survey maps are widely available, especially through booksellers and local newsagents.

# GREATFORD, BARHOLM AND UFFINGTON

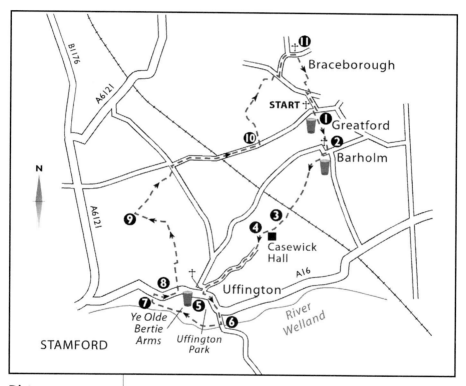

**Distance:**
9¹/₂ miles

**Starting point:**
Greatford.
GR 086118

**Maps: OS Landranger 141 (Kettering and Corby) and
142 (Peterborough), or Explorer 234 (Rutland Water)**

**How to get there:** *Greatford is situated 4 miles north-east
of Stamford in the centre of a triangle of major roads. The
way is clearly signed on all of these: from Tallington on the
A16; Baston on the A15; and Carlby on the A6121. Please
park considerately on the streets in the village.*

THE DELIGHTFUL YE OLDE BERTIE ARMS, UFFINGTON

*L*incolnshire's most striking stone-built villages can be found near to Stamford – itself lauded as 'England's best preserved stone town'. Four of these villages are linked by this full day excursion through the prosperous undulating countryside of south-west Kesteven. A wealth of historical features includes a disused canal, opulent mansions, a thatched inn associated with the local gentry and a curious recurring theme of bygone medical practice.

**Ye Olde Bertie Arms** is a Grade II listed inn dating back to 1681 – almost to the time when the Bertie family first settled at Uffington Hall. In fine weather, the forecourt is the perfect spot to sit and admire the huge overhanging thatched roof. The elevated ambience is reflected in the menu; it all sounds mouth-watering and a bit special. Steaks are a speciality and the accompanying sauces include whisky and blue cheese; a morello cherry sauce arrives with the honey roast duck. Seabass and swordfish are among a good range of fish dishes, but if something less exotic is what you're looking for the

Bertie burgers might be a good choice. Traditional roasts are added to the lunch menu on Sunday, and tempting home-made sponges and pies will fill any room you have left. This is all helped along with a perfect pint of Adnams or Fuller's London Pride, and Caffreys, Stella Artois and Guinness are also on offer.

In addition to usual opening times the Bertie Arms stays open all afternoon at weekends, and meals are available between noon and 2 pm, and between 6.30 pm and 9 pm in the evenings (noon to 9.30 pm Saturdays and Sundays).

**Telephone:** *01780 763834*
*The Hare and Hounds in Greatford also serves excellent food, but no meals are available at the Five Horseshoes in Barholm.*

 *The Walk*

The treatment of ill health is a recurring theme of this walk. Greatford became the home of Dr Francis Willis, who famously cured King George III of his insanity. He established a private asylum at Greatford Hall, and Shillingthorpe Hall, now vanished, was also used by him as a psychiatric hospital.
Braceborough's spa, too, is no more; the spa house, hotel, and railway station have all gone, although the mineral waters still flow.

Undoubtedly one of South Kesteven's most dazzling jewels, Greatford boasts a unique legacy in its collection of curious stone sculptures carved by Major Fitzwilliam, the owner of Greatford Hall in the 1930s, which are now dotted around the village centre. Look for his coronets, mushrooms, and elephant, to name but a few.

① Set out along the public footpath to the left of the **Hare and Hounds** in **Greatford**. Paved initially as it passes a farmyard, your way becomes a simple grass path as far as the first stile and then a clear path through two cornfields; cross a green metal footbridge between them and keep the stone church tower ahead as your goal. This footpath joins a fenced farm track as it approaches the churchyard; here two stone stiles lead you through the gravestones to a lane.

② Turn right along the lane into the little village of **Barholm** and turn left into the tiny lane leading down to a delightful stone pub named the **Five Horseshoes**. On arriving at grand, stone-built **Barholm Hall**, branch right onto the rough track behind the stone outbuildings; this

11

arcs to a gate, and beyond that pursues a clear field path to reach the edge of the wood now ahead of you. Where the wood narrows to a mere hedgerow, go through the gate on your left. Another clear path then leads through the cornfield towards a raised railway track. (This is the main GNER line from London, and trains scream along here at speeds of more than 100 mph – exciting to stand and watch but the utmost care must be exercised during the crossing.) Through the kissing-gate on the far side of the railtrack, locate a narrow footbridge on the left, over which two more diagonal cornfield tracks guide you to the perimeter of a wood with an altogether more cultivated feel to it.

③ The lane into the grounds here passes a large square dovecote and a thatched stone house, and you realize that this is not a wood, it is a park. Tall clipped hedges, exotic trees, and high walls confine you to your route, and, passing between the grandest of stone gate piers, you can now look back over the ha-ha to your left for the best view of **Casewick Hall** itself. This ivy-clad showpiece of stepped gables and mullioned windows was built in the Gothic style by Sir William Trollope in 1789. Continue through the park to leave via a pair of gate pillars almost identical to those near the hall.

④ The country lane now leads you for almost a mile as far as **Uffington**, another compact village of fine stone houses. Turn right into **School Lane** and then go into the yard of **St Michael's church**. Having examined the church and its lofty crocketed spire, leave the churchyard by the grand gates on the main road, where you cannot fail to be impressed by the splendid entrance to **Uffington Hall** opposite you.

*The Berties moved to Uffington in 1670. The hall, a smaller version of Belton House, was completed eleven years later but was tragically destroyed by fire in 1904. Only two visible features remain. The dramatic gate piers opposite the church are quite the best in the county, and on top of another set of stone pillars at the park's eastern entrance are a pair of alarming staring figures, naked apart from their crowns.*

⑤ Turn left along the main road for a short distance, passing a stone lion's head fountain, erected for Queen Victoria's diamond jubilee in 1897, to arrive at **Ye Olde Bertie Arms** on your left. On leaving the **Bertie Arms**, continue along the main road to a turning on the right signed for **Barnack**, where twin stone lodges flank another pair of impressive gates guarding **Uffington Park**. This lane leads steeply down to a narrow old stone bridge over the **River Welland**, but before the bridge turn right at a green gate onto a signed footpath.

⑥ The next section is a magical trip through a tunnel of tangled trees and hedges, the pastures on your left sloping down to the **River Welland**, while to your right runs a curious overgrown channel. This was the course of the **Welland Navigational Canal**. From the former canal bank views open up every so often to the spectacular turrets and towers of **Burleigh House** across the Welland meadows, and there are glimpses of the spires of **Stamford** in front of you.

*The Welland Navigational Canal, linking Stamford to the east coast, was active from 1673 to 1863, when the burgeoning rail network rendered it redundant. The Welland itself, running parallel, had been a trade route since the Stone Age. Roman and medieval remains have also been found here, underlining the strategic importance of the nearby confluence of the Welland and Gwash.*

⑦ At a stile next to the stone remnants of a lock wall, a footbridge carries you over the canal, from where the path leads alongside a fence and over two more stiles to the main road. Cross the road carefully and head right, towards **Uffington** once more, until you come to a black gate on the left, just past a house named **Park View**. You will realize that you are almost back to the church in **Uffington**, but the circuit you have just completed is a high point of the walk which should not be missed

⑧ The black gate takes you onto a path which passes through a short, difficult stretch of undergrowth before it emerges as a good open field-edge track ahead of you. This track extends for a full mile, with a dog-leg midway. A public footpath sign then ushers you onto a lesser path on the left, which you follow for a twisting half-mile, keeping the

CASEWICK HALL

hedge on your left. Finally you emerge onto a shaded green lane close to **Cobbs Nook Farm**.

⑨ Turn right and follow this lane along Lincolnshire's extreme western boundary, past **Seven Acre Wood**, to a metalled road. Turn left here and almost immediately right (signed **Greatford**), and continue along this road for another mile. When you see two rows of large sycamores at a footpath sign on your left, cross the stile and walk up the avenue between them.

⑩ This is a rich landscape, and when the track twists to cross a river at a bridge strewn with masonry you become aware that this was once the sumptuous park of **Shillingthorpe Hall**. Soon a gate takes you into a short wooded passage, emerging from which you strike out to the right on an obvious path, targetting the gap between two woods. On the other side of the gap, continue diagonally across the next two fields (the path is clearly defined), cross a plank bridge, and then follow a lovely twisting field-edge path as far as a road. Continue

straight over the road onto a narrower lane which bends to the left before leading into the peaceful village of **Braceborough**, which was once a thriving spa resort.

⑪ Turn right in the centre of the village at an iron beacon-holder, seasonally overflowing with colourful flowers. This charming lane to nowhere winds past stone mansions and the ancient broach spire of the church to a range of low, stone cottages at the Manor House. However, before the church, look for an unsigned side road to the right, which passes close to a thatched building. Along here, when the road crooks left, go through the gate straight in front of you; then cross a stile, a meadow and another stile, to find yourself back in open country. The path ahead is clear, but, over a wooden footbridge, shuffles briefly to the right before continuing in its original direction. Soon your path merges with the road coming in from the right, and you are guided back into the heart of **Greatford**, with the **Hare and Hounds** almost straight ahead of you.

*Date walk completed:*

# CROWLAND AND THE RIVER WELLAND

TRINITY BRIDGE, CROWLAND

**Distance:**
11 miles

**Starting point:**
St Mary's church in Cowbit.
GR 260180

Maps: OS Landranger 131 (Boston and Spalding), or Explorer 235 (Wisbech and Peterborough)

**How to get there:** *Cowbit lies on the A1073, 3¹/₂ miles south of Spalding. There is parking in the lay-by in front of the church or along the streets behind the main road.*

15

*C*rowland is a conundrum. It is mysterious and forgotten, and its history adds to its sense of isolation and eeriness. Neither the wealth of stone-built Deepings nor the Dutch elegance of the nearby fen towns is in evidence here. Yet the town possesses the county's finest ecclesiastical ruin, the haunting wreck of a Benedictine abbey, challenged only by Thornton Abbey in the county's extreme north. As you follow this straightforward but exhilarating walk, mainly on raised grassy river banks, the abbey is never out of view – a distinctive grey silhouette when seen through morning mist, and breathtaking when illuminated as darkness falls.

Whether **The Olde Bridge Inn** acquired its name from nearby Fen Bridge or the medieval Trinity Bridge in the heart of the town is unclear. What is certain is that the landlords are maintaining the reputation for fine food enjoyed by this pub for many years. Somewhat hidden below the raised Welland river bank and dwarfed by the adjacent white water-tower, the pub is surprisingly inviting inside. Low wooden beams and pillars have been added, and an array of copper and brass implements adorn the white walls and ledges. Several menus for differing requirements run side by side. The fare on all of them is excellent. The specials board changes on a weekly basis. Lamb and mint suet pudding might appear and, if ostrich steak and redcurrant sauce does not, then bison or kangaroo steak probably will. At lunchtime on Sundays roast dinners replace the standard menus. Lovers of good ales will be pleased to find Old Speckled Hen and Abbot ales alongside the usual Tetley, Carlsberg lager, and Guinness.

The Bridge is closed on Mondays but otherwise observes normal licensing hours, remaining open all afternoon on Fridays and Sundays. Meals are served from 12 noon to 2.30 pm at lunchtime and start again between 5 pm and 6 pm in the evenings.

**Telephone:** *01733 210567*

 ## *The Walk*

① From the sturdy stone tower of **St Mary's church** in Cowbit (pronounced cubbit), proceed south along the main road for half a mile in the direction of **Crowland**. On reaching the last house on the left, look to the right to discover a firm

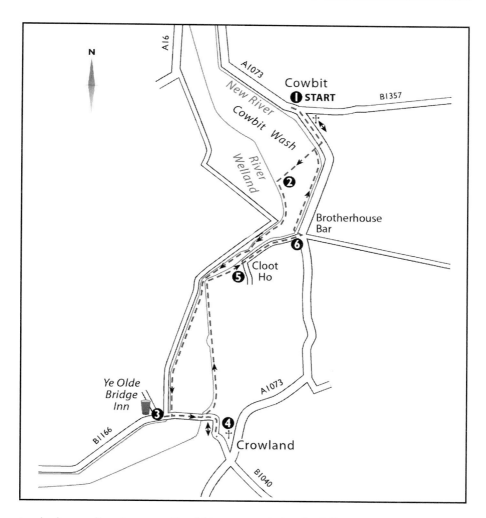

track descending to cross **Cowbit Wash**. This is **Bell Row Drove**, which downgrades to a grass track midway before arriving at the levee guarding the **River Welland**.

② The next section could not be more straightforward: turn left here and simply follow the high bank above the broad slow waters of the Welland for 3½ miles, with only a few stiles and gates interrupting your progress.

*Close by, swans glide and herons*

17

*swoop – even owls may want to share the riverside experience. Views over the flat fenlands extend forever, broken by patches of trees receding into the distance and emphasizing the vastness of the outlook. Overhead, huge skies change continually and are particularly dramatic when tinted by the low light of sunset.*

Keeping your gaze focused on the grim grey outline of the ruined abbey in **Crowland**, you at last emerge onto a roadside next to **Fen Bridge** and close to a colossal octagonal white water-tower and, of course, **The Olde Bridge Inn**.

③ Leave the pub, cross **Fen Bridge** once more, and follow the raised causeway alongside **The Lake**, a long fishpond covered in lilypads

and set in lawns shaded by a row of willows. At the T-junction, turn left, follow the right-hand curve, and turn right into **North Street**, to enter the little town of **Crowland**, where two important medieval sites must be inspected.

*Here is Lincolnshire's most spectacular ruin. Nothing remains of the original wattle-walled abbey founded in the 8th century. The handsome relic we see today dates mainly from the 1420s, but some Norman dog-tooth work can still be seen. Nearby, the oddity that is Trinity Bridge was built in the 14th century. The three stone arches spanned the rivers that met in the centre of Crowland, and the bridge was described by Gough as 'the greatest curiosity in Britain if not in Europe'. The rivers have since been diverted, but the wide streets leading from the bridge indicate their positions.*

④ Leave Crowland by **North Street**, but this time continue straight over **Kemp Street** into **North Bank**. This firm track passes houses and stables on the right before a gate leads

CROYLAND ABBEY AT CROWLAND

you onto a more grassy trail. Do not ascend **Wash Bank** to your left; the going is tough and progress is barred by fences. Continue until the bank makes a wide semi-circular detour around a fishpond lined with bulrushes. Through a gate, you may now climb the bank to reveal once more the far reaching fenscape and the New River below. At a pumping station where the Welland comes almost alongside, choose between maintaining the high ground or dropping to a better track below. Both take you through a gate leading onto the lawns of a farmstead named **Cloot House**.

⑤ Join the metalled road in front of you and continue in your original direction, with the New River still to your left. Less than a mile along this lane you reach the junction with the A1073 at **Brotherhouse Bar**. Here look carefully on the verge to your right to see a mounted stone tablet, the shaft of St Guthlac's cross. It stands in proud isolation in the winter but in summer tends to disappear in the vegetation.

*This 12th century relic is a*

*boundary marker for Croyland Abbey. The inscription means 'This rock, I say, is Guthlac's upmost bound'. St Guthlac, a hermit monk seeking a life of solitude, had landed at Crowland in 699 with his boatman Tatwin and a servant. Crowland at that time was merely a deserted muddy islet, or crulande. The simplicity and holiness of Guthlac's life earned him a reputation as a spiritual counsellor. Ethelbald, the future king of Mercia, sought sanctuary with him and, following the death and canonization of the monk, it was Ethelbald who laid the foundation stones of the abbey in 716.*

⑥ From the cross, split away from the main road and take the track leading down to a wooden bridge over the New River. Turn right onto the drove track on the other side of the river. Now follow this open grassy track for more than a mile until, at the second of two trees, you recognize **Bell Row Drove**. Go up to the main road, turn left, and your starting point in **Cowbit** is now only $1/2$ mile to the north.

*Date walk completed:*

# THE FENLAND AROUND SPALDING

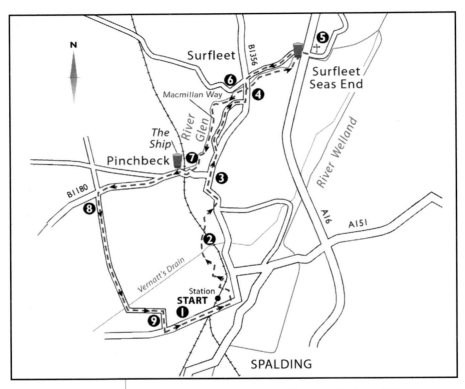

**Distance:**
11 miles

**Starting point:**
*Spalding Market Place.*
*GR 247226*

Maps: **OS 131 (Boston and Spalding), or Explorer 249 (Spalding and Holbeach)**

**How to get there:** *Spalding is easily located on the A16, in the south of the county, and Market Place itself is central. Seek a parking spot in the nearby streets or follow the signs to one of many public car parks in and around the town centre.*

SURFLEET SEAS END

*H*ere is an expedition contrasting the hustle and bustle of Spalding's Market Place with the peace and solitude of the meandering River Glen, disturbed only by the gentle ripples of the occasional boat passing lazily by. Along the riverside you will come across an award winning thatched pub and a precarious medieval spire. The walk is level throughout, and mainly on firm grassy paths and quiet lanes, apart from the start and finish of the walk in Spalding itself. Any spare time should be devoted to an exploration of Ayscoughee Hall or any of Spalding's other historic houses and museums.

**The Ship** was originally built in 1670 to serve the boatmen on their way to and from Bourne on the River Glen. Some of the pub's original beams are said to be timbers from the hull of one of their vessels. Today, the Ship is in a secluded spot by the River Glen, sandwiched between road and railway, but still as pretty as a picture. Willows shade the grassy riverbank, while ivy creeps over the low thatch of the whitewashed inn. Inside, the bar area is

21

divided into three small rooms, where locals gather and chat, while most meals are served in the spacious restaurant, whose doors open straight onto the lawns behind. You may take some time to choose from the extensive menu; here is everything from ham, leek, and potato pie to pork fillets Rainfort, served with a cream, wine, and horseradish sauce. There are lots of fish dishes in delicious-sounding sauces – halibut in white wine sauce is one – and a wild mushroom lasagne is one of six vegetarian choices. The desserts, too, are home-made and sound very exotic. Brandy snaps are filled with tiramisu ice cream and the Pinchbeck surprise is filled with – well, that's a surprise! A separate snack menu will be sufficient for many, with a good range of baguette and jacket potato fillings. On Sundays, a special roast lunch is available, and for this you should book in advance. A guest beer such as London Pride always accompanies the Courage Directors and Theakston's Mild on the bar, along with the expected draught beers and lagers.

The Ship is open every day, serving meals from 12 noon to 2 pm and from 5.30 pm to 9 pm. On Saturday and Sunday evenings meals may start a little later.

**Telephone:** *01775 723792*
*The Mermaid at Surfleet enjoys a similar reputation for fine food, while taverns and eating establishments abound in the centre of Spalding.*

# The Walk

Before the Dissolution, the monastery at Spalding was one of Lincolnshire's wealthiest and played an important part in the reclamation of the fens and marshes. The prosperity of Spalding increased with the thriving wool trade, and it was a wool merchant, Richard Alwyn, who built beautiful Ayscoughee Hall, which now houses a museum dedicated to the history of the reclamation of the fens. Since it was first built in the 15th century, the hall has frequently been extended, and an exploration of its rooms, exhibitions, and gardens is to be recommended. The same is true of its neighbour, the church of St Mary and St Nicholas, first built in 1284. The many subsequent additions have led to its present cathedral-like proportions.

① **Spalding's Market Place** is lined with impressive Victorian facades, and there are even older inns which can be admired as you stroll up to **New Road**. Turn right here and then left into **Pinchbeck Road** for a short distance, turning left again when you reach **King's Road**. Just before King's Road swings to the left towards a colossal square water-tower, cross a rather rusty iron footbridge ahead of you leading over the railway to another busy road, which you follow to the right. Next, take a left turn into **Park Row**, and, in 200 yards, look for a narrow signed footpath on your right, which takes you through to disused brick premises on **Woolramwygate**. Turn left here. In a few yards, a turning to the right takes you into **Two Plank Lane**, but, instead of following the curving road into an area of new housing, take the old track straight ahead of you which leads you away from the houses to cross **Vernatt's Drain** at **Two Plank Bridge**.

② On joining **Blue Gowt Lane**, continue ahead, and, over a level crossing, turn right into **Market Way**, which takes you back to the main road to **Pinchbeck**. Now simply follow the main road to the left for almost a mile to enter the village of **Pinchbeck** and enjoy its best features. Past the delightful rectory, the village's crowning glory is the grand Gothic church of St Mary, best seen when framed by the

arched stone entrance to the churchyard.

③ Pass two inns (outside the Bull, a replica set of the old village stocks can be seen) to reach a small green on the left, on which is mounted the Pinchbeck village sign. Here, adorning a green iron bench, are ornately crafted daffodil blooms, also made of iron and painted bright yellow. The road branching to the left here is **Crossgates Lane**, one of a network between the main road and the **River Glen**. **Crossgates Lane** takes you straight into **Bacon's Lane** and then into **Cuckoo Lane** before it rejoins the highway leading you left towards **Surfleet** and the approaching spire of St Laurence's church, leaning alarmingly.

④ Just in front of the metal bridge, look to your right for a gap in the hedgerow opening onto a pleasing

TWO PLANK BRIDGE, SPALDING

THE FENLAND AROUND SPALDING

stretch of parkland alongside the riverbank. The shade of the willows in the park soon gives way to the open fenscape again, and you continue along the banktop path above the **River Glen**, now on the **Macmillan Way**. A mile later, you cross to the opposite bank by passing underneath the new road, ascending a flight of steps, crossing the river on the same bridge as the traffic, and then passing under the road once more to emerge at the **Riverside Hotel**. (At this point you could elect to continue along the riverside for a further mile to visit **Surfleet Seas End**, where the Welland, the Glen, and Vernatt's Drain all converge. Here holiday bungalows and neat lawns line the riverbank, guarded by the huge sluice gate, but outside the sluice is a muddy tidal stretch where the timbers of disused jetties stand rotting.)

⑤ As you head back along this road, the Glen meanders away from your route and then back again, often just behind the houses lining the street, until it reaches the gravity-defying spire of **Surfleet** again.

*The leaning tower and spire of St Laurence's church in Surfleet bear witness to the silty soil on which the foundations stand. At the summit, the deviation from the perpendicular of 6'4'' is greater than that of the Leaning Tower of Pisa! Inside, too, mighty buttresses shore up the steadily sinking stonework, and a number of good monuments make a visit particularly worthwhile.*

⑥ Cross the metal bridge at the handsome **Mermaid Inn** and locate a stile on your right, where a finger post directs you towards Pinchbeck station, long since vanished, of course. This charming grassy path now carries you for more than a mile along the winding **River Glen**, sometimes on top of the levee, sometimes on a broad terrace between the banktop and the water. An atmosphere of peace and solitude presides, interrupted only by an eerie patch of decaying woodland in a swamp known as **Cricket Bat Willows**, which is positively spooky at twilight. Over a road, the path becomes more constricted as it passes the wall of a renovated flax mill, but you should remain as close as possible to the river throughout. Eventually, just beyond a railway track crossed with great care via two stiles, you find yourself in the grounds of a thatched inn – you have reached **The Ship**.

⑦ Leaving **The Ship** by the main gate, turn right to cross the Glen; then turn immediately left onto a grassy riverside path, still following the **Macmillan Way**. The road soon rejoins you and accompanies you past the **Rose Cottage Tropical Forest** and a swathe of land named **Pinchbeck Wood**, which has been newly planted with native trees such as alder and crack willow as part of a Woodland Trust conservation project. Continue above the wide river for about a mile. Both banks are studded with handsome brick farms and houses, while swans and various species of waterfowl glide amongst the reeds and bulrushes in the water below. At **Money Bridge** cross the Glen and continue along **Money Bridge Lane** away from the river, now on another recognized route: the **Brown Fen Waterway Trail**. (Visible another half mile along the river is the white ogee cap of Glen Mill, a windmill surmounted by a curious painted globe, itself crowned by a galleon.)

⑧ **Money Bridge Lane** is pleasant enough, with good views of Spalding through a row of ivy covered horse chestnut trees on your left. Some 1$\frac{1}{2}$ straight miles along here, the road bends to the right when it meets **Vernatt's Drain**, but your route is over **Jobson's Bridge**, the wooden footbridge spanning this drainage channel. Now follow the track halfway round the farm on the left, before shooting off onto the field-edge path running alongside a lesser dyke towards a gathering of greenhouses.

⑨ Clear a stile past the greenhouses, turn right into **Monk's House Lane**, and follow it all the way to a set of traffic lights, glimpsing on your left **Monk's House** itself, an L-shaped Tudor building with later Jacobean additions. Turn left at the lights and simply follow **Bourne Road** into the increasing hubbub of Spalding, going over the railway line and through **Sheepmarket**; the busy **Market Place** soon appears on your right once more.

*There is no escaping the Dutch influence in Spalding. Long elegant terraces and larger mansions bear the hallmark of one of Spalding's major trading partners and the source of much expertise for the gradual fen reclamation programme. This entire corner of the county even bears the name Holland and tulips, of course, have become synonymous with Spalding. The annual tulip parade has taken place through the town every May since 1959.*

Date walk completed:

# EDENHAM AND CASTLE BYTHAM

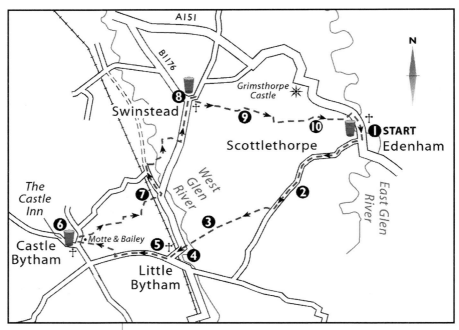

**Distance:**
11½ miles

**Starting point:**
Edenham.
GR 062218

Maps: OS Landranger 130 (Grantham), or Explorer 247
(Grantham) and Explorer 248 (Bourne and Heckington)

**How to get there:** Edenham is found along the A151
3 miles west of Bourne, in the direction of Colsterworth.
You can park near the church, either on the main road or
in the streets behind.

CASTLE BYTHAM

*I* had never seen a wild deer. Despite Lincolnshire's many signs warning me to beware of them, I assumed their existence to be mere myth. But while devising this expedition I have regularly been delighted by groups of these wonderful beasts, sometimes grazing quietly in the distance, sometimes seen at close quarters emerging at speed from the woods. These woods are just one part of this magical trip, which twice crosses the parklands of Grimsthorpe. Contrast the sensational views across the lake to stately Grimsthorpe Castle with the atmospheric earthworks of the vanished medieval fort in Castle Bytham, where a small stone inn has an unusually warm welcome for you.

Next to the narrow lane leading to the church and at the summit of the steep small green, the old stone walls of the **Castle Inn** enjoy the village's most envied position. Inside, flowers are everywhere, and the old stonework of the walls has been left exposed. There is a real fire and the small window bays form two lovely alcoves. The pub has a well deserved reputation for good food and good beer. All the food is prepared on the premises and the menu regularly changes. The menus have a refined feel that matches the surroundings, but the separate bar menu does offer pastas, salads, a delicious steak and kidney pudding, and lamb shank with a red wine and rosemary gravy. Venison haunch and Lincolnshire rabbit pie appear on the main menu, while vegetarians might choose between the parsnip and sweet potato bake and the mushroom and brandy sauce parcel. Lavish roasts are added to the choices on Sundays. Whatever your taste, the cook will try and accommodate you, and this includes arranging smaller meals for youngsters. For real ale lovers, there is Cooking and Ten-Fifty from the Grainstore Brewery in nearby Rutland.

The Castle serves meals from 12 noon to 2.30 pm and begins again at 7 pm. Early evening promotions on Tuesdays and Wednesdays start at 5.30 pm. The inn is closed altogether on Mondays.

**Telephone:** *01780 410504*
*Elsewhere on the walk, the pubs in Edenham (the Five Bells) and Little Bytham (the Willoughby Arms) also provide excellent meals, and the Fox and Hounds is just a few yards along the road from the Castle.*

---

 # The Walk

① From the shade of the huge cedar in **Edenham churchyard**, set off left along the main road. Past the bridge over the **East Glen river**, turn right into **Scottlethorpe Road**, soon passing Elm Row, an imposing terrace of estate cottages built of banded stone in the 1890s. Follow the undulating lane through **Scottlethorpe**, an interesting jumble of farms and stone cottages, until, having passed a disused quarry, the metalled surface bends to the left at the top of a hill. Your direction, however, does not deviate and you continue along the chalky track

entering the woods ahead of you, which later merges with Lord Willoughby's one-time private railway line.

*Lord Willoughby of Grimsthorpe Castle was a progressive landowner. Already using steam engines to plough his land when the GNER brought the railway to nearby Little Bytham in 1852, he decided to link his park with the main line by laying a private track across the estate to Edenham. Part of your route follows the old track bed near Scottlethorpe, and a weighbridge cabin still stands in the farmyard at the end of the walk in Edenham. (The original route is clearly marked on the*

*OS Explorer map, but not on the Landranger map.) It was at Little Bytham in 1938 that the Mallard achieved the steam locomotive record speed of 126 mph.*

② In half a mile, at the second public footpath sign, turn right off the track to follow the left-hand edge of a tiny plantation. Beyond the plantation, a track coming in from the left accompanies you into the woods in front of you, now deep in the heart of the Grimsthorpe Estate. Turn left onto the main track winding through the woodland, and then right at its next bend, to pursue a grass track along the southern edge of **Kennel Plantation**. Past two fishing ponds the path continues between two arable fields to a grand meeting of ways at **New Buildings**: six avenues and ridings radiate from this point. The 'new buildings' have in fact been flattened, leaving only a courtyard and a cottage nearby.

③ Approach this cottage and then wheel to the left. A few yards along the avenue now in front of you, a clear yellow arrow indicates your way along a grassy swathe to the right – this is **Bytham Riding** – and the spire of **Little Bytham church** comes immediately into view ahead of you. At the foot of a hill, exit these privileged surroundings via a heavy iron gate, and continue on the track ahead over a wooden bridge, through a gate, and finally into **Little Bytham**.

④ If time is your enemy, you can be through **Little Bytham** quickly enough by simply following the road you are on through the village – under the gigantic brick arches of the Great Northern Railway and past Bees village shop, seemingly unchanged inside since the coming of the railway. But I recommend a more thorough exploration of this intriguing village's features. In front of the mighty arches, turn left onto a track leading down to a ford; here a concrete footbridge and a stile take you into a large meadow. At the far end of this tapering meadow, a kissing-gate leads towards another railway arch. Your progress through this arch seems to be barred as the **West Glen River** rushes underneath its entire span. However, an ingenious catwalk mounted on an iron gantry midway up the wall of the arch enables you to continue to the road beyond. Turn right onto this road and right again at the T-junction, passing under two more railway arches before arriving at a stream near the centre of the village. Do not cross the stream but branch onto a narrow shaded lane along the left-hand bank. Crossing the stream by a footbridge next to a ford, the lane leads you up to the church (dedicated uniquely to St Medard

29

and St Gildard), at which you turn left and leave the village.

⑤ Walk along this road for almost a mile until, just past a renovated stone building on your left, you come to a signed footpath at a stile and gate on the right. The track leads down to another gate at the entrance to the now disused **Thunderbolt Pit**, in front of which you turn left and follow the field-edge path as far as a stile. Now take a diagonal path to the opposite corner of the next meadow, where an improving surface leads past the most idyllically sited cricket pitch, all the while enjoying developing views over the village of **Castle Bytham**. A gate and a short lane later, you find yourself in the centre of the village, where, to your left, a steep village green leads your gaze up to

the hilltop church tower – and, nestling between the two, the stone façade of the **Castle Inn**.

*Though the steep grassy ramparts of the castle still dominate the village, Castle Bytham must once have been an even more impressive spectacle when stone walls and towers guarded this fortification – maybe even as grand as indicated by the Castle Inn sign! First constructed by Odo, the half brother of William the Conqueror, the castle yielded to a major siege in 1221, when the tenant, William de Fortibus, rebelled against the young Henry III. The castle was rebuilt after the siege but disappears mysteriously from records beyond 1400, though in 1540 the historian John Leland declared that there 'yet remayne great walles of buildinge'.*

**THE RIVER GLEN AT LITTLE BYTHAM**

⑥ Down the hill from the pub, follow the stream along the main road of this most attractive stone village. At the quaint duckpond, look across the main road for a footbridge and a stile leading into the actual precincts of the castle earthworks. A sign forbids closer inspection, but the impressive ramparts can be well surveyed from these close quarters. To your left, a stile leads into a steep open field, where a row of white waymarkers guides you up the hill to a stile, all the time offering the best views yet over the castle and the village. Over the stile turn left and make a beeline for **Lawn Wood**, whose charming perimeter path you follow for the next half-mile. Where the wood ends, turn left by passing through two hedgerows, to continue around the wood once more to a track near to a tall pylon. (Do not attempt to pursue the diagonal path shown on the Ordnance Survey map.) Turn right onto the track, which twists past a group of derelict buildings before descending towards the village of **Creeton**, its squat spire now prominent in the middle distance.

⑦ Do not enter the village, however, but turn left at the road junction below the railway bridge and follow this lane until it turns under the railtrack. At this bend in the road, continue straight ahead along a good track known as **The Drift**. A short distance further on, a public footpath sign ushers you away from The Drift and down the hillside to your right. A clear footpath winds through this lovely valley to a wooden footbridge over the West Glen. Over two more stiles you begin to regain height as you

hug the edge of **Croakhill Plantation** for another half-mile. Look for a yellow arrow directing you onto a better track on your right and thence to **Creeton Farm**. Reach the road via the field path to the left of the farm and not through the farmyard itself. Turn left and stroll along this road into the fine stone-built village of **Swinstead**.

⑧ At the church tower, embattled and pinnacled, turn right to pass an inn called **The Windmill**. (I have found no record of the village ever possessing one!) Now turn right again into **Park Road** to enjoy some of the village's best buildings, making sure not to enter the gated park of **Swinstead Hall** ahead but to follow the tarmac lane to the left. Now glance left to view a tall summer pavilion, a most unexpected find in these fields.

*Swinstead's pavilion, unmistakably a creation of Sir John Vanbrugh, was built in the 1720s as a visual link with Grimsthorpe Castle. Despite its Grade1 listed status, it was abandoned in 1966 and not rescued and restored until 1992. Very tall and elegant, the sturdy central pavilion is flanked by two even taller towers.*

Look for a clearly defined diagonal path across the second field on your left, which leads through a narrow strip of trees onto a good farm track. Along this track, to the right, you soon pass between two woods, and there in front of you, crowning the hillside on the far side of the lake, is the most majestic view of **Grimsthorpe Castle**.

*Illustrious hands indeed have shaped this magnificent view of Grimsthorpe Castle. The lakes, woods, and parkland before you were landscaped in 1722 by Lancelot 'Capability' Brown, while the north front of the castle was spectacularly remodelled in the classical style by Vanbrugh, the creator of Castle Howard and Blenheim Palace. The south side of the castle, however, still incorporates King John's Tower, part of the original 13th century building.*

⑨ On emerging from the woods, fork half right and descend towards the corner of the lake, near to the site of the Cistercian abbey of **Vaudey**, which was founded in 1147 and connected with the early history of the castle. Follow the shore of the lake on the tarmac track as far as a cluster of old oak trees, at which a lesser track branches south. Turn to the left and locate a gate, beyond which a clear track rises up the hillside towards another wood. Here savour the last views back over the lake, the park, and the castle. The path continues directly through a wooded section, emerges onto a field-edge path, which follows the border left and right, before sloping down to a footbridge and a stile.

⑩ The next field is a narrow welcoming pasture divided by a tiny brook, but a sign on the gate into the field after that warns you to beware of the bull; I saw no evidence of anything more threatening than moles! At the far end of this field, a gate leads onto a farmyard track, now following **Lord Willoughby's rail route** again. Only a few yards along this track, negotiate the first of a series of three very high stiles on your right. Two meadows later you find yourself back on the main road, leading past the **Five Bells** on your right to the church in the centre of **Edenham**.

Date walk completed:

# INGOLDSBY, BOOTHBY PAGNELL, ROPSLEY AND HUMBY

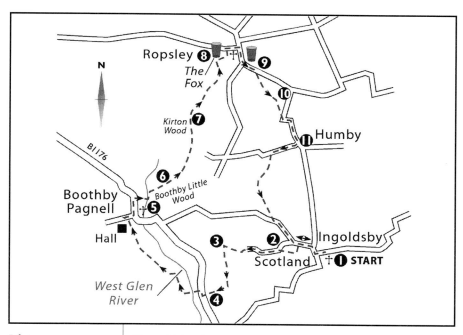

**Distance:**
10 miles

**Starting point:**
*Main Street,*
*Ingoldsby.*
*GR 011301*

**Maps: OS Landranger 130 (Grantham), or Explorer 247 (Grantham) and Explorer 248 (Bourne and Heckington)**

**How to get there:** *Ingoldsby is situated at a meeting of quiet rural lanes, 7 miles south-east of Grantham. From Grantham, head east along the A52, soon branching onto the B1176 at a roundabout. Just past Boothby Pagnell, turn left onto the lane signed for Ingoldsby, which lies 2 miles along here. The village is quiet and you will have no trouble finding a roadside parking spot.*

**THE FOX AT ROPSLEY**

*A*t the end of a hectic working week, here is the perfect walk to get away from it all: a simple but lengthy stroll around Kesteven's stone-built villages, all conducted on delightful rural footpaths and quiet byways. While enjoying the woodlands and gently rolling countryside around the infant River Glen, your day's highlight is a halt at a superior country inn, one of Lincolnshire's oldest and best-known hostelries.

A historic inn in a historic village, **The Ropsley Fox** is a very special place. Built in 1667 and formerly called the Fox's Brush, this was one of three pubs in the village. The attractively irregular contours of the long low stone façade are continued inside. Here the panelled bar area is dark and relaxed, with a large log fire near the centre. It is stacked from floor to ceiling with the most bizarre collection of items, that embraces everything from a boat to a bubble-car! There are tables around the bar, and diners can sit in the huge banquet hall of a restaurant, the conservatory, or even outside on the lawns to the rear. The fare is a cut above the normal. Steaks are a speciality, as are Chinese dishes, and a full range of traditional bar meals is also offered. Here you will find succulent fillets of fresh Grimsby fish, Lord Adey's steak and ale pie and home-made Ropsley burgers. On Sundays roast lunches are also available, and you may be well advised to book. The usual beers and lagers are accompanied by IPA, Deuchars, and a guest ale such as Archer's Blackjack Porter. The Ropsley Fox observes standard opening hours, meals being served between 12 noon and 2 pm, and again from 6.30 pm onwards. It is fortunate that a visit to The Ropsley Fox is such a treat, as it is the only place serving refreshments along the walk.

**Telephone:** *01476 585339*

# The Walk

① From the shade of St Andrew's church towering over Ingoldsby's **Main Street**, head west and admire the large octagonal turret of the neighbouring Manor House. Follow the road as it bends to the right and then to the left before leaving the village in the direction of **Boothby Pagnell**. Halfway down the hill, look for a signed footpath on your left, cross the stile, and head half right across the grass. A dip crossed by 'stepping stones' and a low gate now lead you into a long meadow, in the opposite corner of which another stile takes you back onto tarmac in the tiny hamlet of **Scotland**.

② Follow the lane left past the farm and round a wide bend. Noting **Scotland House**, an immaculate,

stone building guarded by two lofty trimmed yews at its gate, continue to a single bar gate at the end of the lane, which now becomes a path descending through an area of woodland. The path enters an open field briefly before arriving at **Ingoldsby Wood**, the border of which you begin to follow to the left. In only a few yards, you will go into deep woods and onto a bracken-lined path between oak and other native trees on the right and ranks of tall pine and fir on the left. Tracks will try to tempt you left and right, but your route is straight ahead to the edge of the wood.

*In early summer the southern end of Ingoldsby Wood, an area of ancient primary woodland, is spectacularly carpeted with bluebells. Listen for nightingales here and remain alert to spot fallow deer in and around the wood. A circular earthwork, believed to be a rare Iron Age hill-fort, lies at the northern end of the wood.*

③ Now turn left to follow the course of a once important track – the **Mereway** – with the wood and the hedgerow shaping arches and tunnels above your head. A few yards past a footbridge at the limits of the wood, take the clear downhill path to the right, keeping the screening hedge on your left. Your first views now open up of the hall and church in Boothby Pagnell across the valley.

④ At the road turn right, and then soon left at an aluminium gate onto a track descending to cross the infant **West Glen river**. Climb the

opposite bank and pivot to the right at the top of the hillside. Now stroll along this fine open chalky farmtrack for a good mile, enjoying the ever-improving prospect of Boothby Pagnell Hall ahead of you and the gently rolling hills on the far side of the river. On reaching the grounds of the hall, peer through the hedge to steal a sight of the hall itself and the unique Norman manor house; then, at the road, turn right to pass the hall once more and enter the village of **Boothby Pagnell**.

*As you approach the road in Boothby Pagnell, the building on your right, between the hedge and the hall, is the Manor House, dating back to 1200. It is, according to Pevsner's* **Buildings of England**, *simply the most*

**BOOTHBY PAGNELL MANOR HOUSE**

*important small Norman manor house in England. With walls up to four feet thick and originally moated, the house is accessed by a flight of external stone steps. It is now a Grade 1 listed building, and appointments to visit the house can be arranged.*

⑤ Turn left at the handsomely restored church and, at the foot of the hill, climb a stile on your right to enter a delightful narrow meadow – the start of a lengthy excursion through the countryside between here and **Ropsley**. Cross the **West Glen** once more to enter an enclosed track which soon angles to the right and, beyond a series of sheep pens, ascends the hill alongside **Boothby Little Wood**.

⑥ Emerging from this rather difficult section, you find yourself in the corner of a level open cornfield. The true path here is diagonally across the next two fields, but, if the footpath is not in place, you may prefer to continue along the edge of the wood before heading left along the hedgerow to locate a footbridge. Obliquely again, cross the corner of the third field and target a gap in the hedge ahead, on the far side of which you venture to the left to face another large wood: **Kirton Wood**. Ahead of you is a magnificent wide woodland avenue between the towering trunks, and even when this avenue has narrowed to a pathway

the surroundings are no less impressive.

⑦ Stepping from the wood into the daylight, continue in exactly the same direction along a series of field-edge footpaths. Keep the hedge to your right as far as a small pond, beyond which you exchange positions with the hedge. On arriving at a road, turn to the right and look for a new wooden gate on your left leading onto a modest golf course. Cross the course in a straight line and leave by another gate and footbridge. Now back in arable territory, turn right and follow the twisting field-edge path until you spot a gravel drive serving the houses on your right. Cross the gravel and go along a narrow village lane to turn left into **School Lane** and pass the school with its tiny Victorian bell-turret. Now turn left onto the main road and there in front of you is the low stone front of The Ropsley Fox pub.

*St Peter's church in Ropsley displays some of the earliest stonework in the country, with much Anglo-Saxon and Norman work still standing. The fine 15th century porchway was built by Richard Fox, who was born in the village and later became Bishop of Winchester and the founder of Corpus Christi College in Oxford.*

⑧ Turning right out of the pub

37

door, walk into the village and turn right into **High Street** at the marble obelisk, the near-perfect broach spire of St Peter's church now across the green to the side of you. Just past the **Green Man** on the left, espy a public footpath sign on your right ushering you behind a house and then left between the outbuildings, as indicated by the yellow waymarker. Go through a hedged tunnel and carefully across a lawn to find yourself on a track running behind a row of houses. Be sure not to miss a path branching right from this, which you take back into the undergrowth to continue in more or less the same direction.

⑨ When you emerge in a grassy field, the wooded area on your right is actually the remains of a ring dam. From here, three more stiles lead you across two more meadows. On reaching a cultivated field, follow the path half-left to an awkward fenced area in the corner; you are aiming for the stile and footbridge ahead of you, but you may prefer to walk round the electric fence inexplicably erected in your way.

⑩ Having overcome this minor nuisance, cross a stile into a cowfield. A few yards along the hedgerow on your right, another bridge and stile lead you into a very long meadow. Hug the hedge along the lower edge of the meadow to eventually reach a double gate. Through here you turn left onto a firm track. Over a pretty ford, the track leads up to a triangular green surrounded by neat stone houses in the hamlet of **Little Humby**. Facing the green, leave **Little Humby** by the road to the right and walk along here for half a mile, until you arrive at **Humby Hall Farm** in **Great Humby**.

⑪ Just before the farm, a metalled lane forks right, passes the farm and the hall, and leads you to a tiny copse on your left. Past the copse head along a signed footpath through the crops in the next two fields, targeting the red roofs of a range of derelict farm buildings on the skyline ahead. Once at the farm, keep the buildings on your left and join the clear track leading off to the wood. Across a small brook, this lovely undulating lane now leads all the way back to the main road. Turn left here and complete the last mile back into **Ingoldsby** village.

*Date walk completed:*

# CULVERTHORPE LAKE AND THE FORGOTTEN HAMLETS

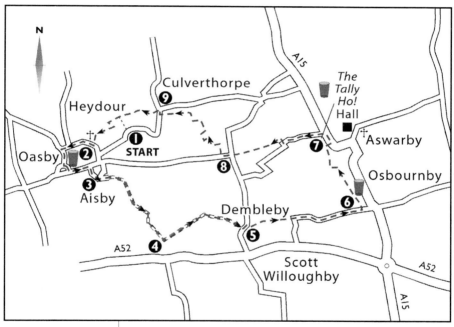

**Distance:**
11 miles

**Starting point:**
*Culverthorpe Lake car park and picnic area. GR 019398*

**Maps: OS Landranger 130 (Grantham), or Explorer 248 (Bourne and Heckington)**

**How to get there:** *From the A15, 4 miles south of Sleaford, two signed lanes lead off to the right in the direction of the village of Swarby. From Swarby continue west for 2 more miles to Culverthorpe. The car park by the lake is clearly indicated just past the village.*

CULVERTHORPE IN THE SNOW

*T*his eventful ramble through the timeless landscape between Sleaford and Grantham is laden with fascinating historical features. A series of forgotten stone hamlets, some linked by ancient green lanes, is explored. One was built where a medieval castle once stood and another has an inn rich in hunting tradition, which is a real treat to spur you onwards. The finale of your journey is a stunning chateau-like hall, once the seat of a branch of Sir Isaac Newton's family.

**The Tally Ho!** cannot be missed as you travel south from Sleaford towards Bourne. Built of local stone, the imposing gables and tall chimneys of this 17th century building are an arresting sight, and, apart from the adjoining stables (now guest accommodation), the inn stands alone, away from the village to whose estate it still belongs. But the interior conveys an entirely different atmosphere: intimate and welcoming, with huge open log fires, stone walls throughout, and lots of comfortable sofas and old seats. A restaurant area has been developed to the rear, but you will probably prefer to eat in the bar, surrounded by pictures and maps reflecting the inn's hunting heritage and its connections with the Belvoir Hunt. As you sit and listen in to the discussions of the locals, select your meal from the mouth-watering choices on the menu and specials board. The food is all of extremely high quality and leans heavily on locally bought produce; Lincolnshire sausages and mash is a favourite, and you may find venison steaks from nearby Threekingham. More unusual choices include sizzlers – stir-fried dishes served on a hot trivet. The desserts sound equally delicious; try saying no to the banana and toffee pancakes! Excellent beers are also available, Everard's Tiger, Adnams, and Beacon Smooth among them. The Tally Ho! is open every day and meals are available between 12 noon and 2 pm at lunchtime and from 6 pm to 9.30 pm in the evening.

**Telephone:** *01529 455205*
*The Houblon Arms in Oasby is the only other place on the route where refreshments can be bought.*

 # The Walk

① Having first explored the lakeside picnic area and located a seat in the form of a large fish carved from a lime trunk by Anthony Holloway in 1991, set out along the delightful hedged causeway between the two lakes. The track sweeps up the hillside and past a farm on the right. Through one gate but before a second, a grassy bridleway shoots to the left, a hedge running to its right. At its end, angle left along a shorter, tree-lined track, and, when you are offered a choice of pathways, go left again and follow what becomes a narrow path around the edge of a field. When a surfaced track crosses

your route, identify a footbridge opposite, leading you over a stile and into a large meadow. With the handsome church spire in **Heydour** as your objective, cross the meadow diagonally and exit via a gateway on the right. Across a smaller field, you are now led to a low wall at the back of the churchyard, and beyond the yard is a lane in the centre of the hollow sheltering the hidden hamlet of **Heydour**.

*Though secluded in its valley, Heydour, you will find, has several intriguing features. The lofty church contains a wealth of impressive monuments to the Newton family from Culverthorpe Hall. Next to it the statue of a young musician in a niche above*

41

*the rectory door is reputed to be the only remnant of Heydour Castle. The castle itself is also passed on the walk, though only the earthworks covering the foundations remain visible, an indication of how this once significant settlement has declined since medieval times.*

② Turn right and climb out of **Heydour**, passing the barely discernible earthworks of the former castle bailey to your right. At a T-junction turn left and enter the neighbouring village of **Oasby**. At a delightful inn called the **Houblon Arms**, turn left and follow the narrow lane between some of the village's best stone buildings to a main road. Walk left along this road for about a quarter of a mile, looking out for a public footpath sign on your right. The footpath is a shortcut past a playing field into the last of this trinity of villages: **Aisby**.

③ Join the lane running down the hill below the **Millennium Green**, around which most of Aisby's houses are grouped. Ignore the road on your left leading back up the hill and continue into **Green Lane**, which takes you past more fine stone buildings before leaving the village. **Green Lane** quickly deteriorates into a deeply rutted track but re-emerges from a wooded section true to its claim as one of

THE WELCOMING TALLY HO! INN AT ASWARBY

Lincolnshire's 'green lanes', flanked by wide grassy verges and hedged on each side. Now stroll on for over a mile, adhering strictly to the hedged lane and finally reaching a clear meeting of lanes, at which you turn left, as indicated by a red arrow.

④ You are still on **Green Lane**, which slowly improves as it approaches the remote hamlet of **Dembleby**, passing en route a particularly striking stone farmhouse. Past the tiny church of St Lucia, do not follow the road round to the left, but locate a signed bridleway along the open hillside to the right of the unnamed house in front of you.

*Dembleby's tiny church of St Lucia was rebuilt in 1869 but incorporates some original medieval fragments. One of these is the pillar piscina, a decorated stone basin now used as the font and acclaimed by Pevsner as the country's finest.*

⑤ This track guides you to a road above a wayside church in **Scott Willoughby**, and a further half mile in the same direction brings you into **Osbournby**, the most substantial of the walk's villages. In the heart of **Osbournby** you find yourself in a spacious triangular square – if such a thing exists – a market place surrounded by a

wealth of diverse brick and stone buildings, but without a market.

⑥ **North Street** leads out of the corner of the square on your left and continues unerringly north until, as a track, it reaches a hilltop plantation. Did you spot the word JUBILEE picked out in huge shrubbery letters on the steepest slope of the hillside? Through a gap between the trees, breathtaking views now open up past an isolated copse of Scots pine and over Aswarby's park and church to a fenland horizon pricked by innumerable noble Gothic spires. The path skirts the plantation and, at the foot of the hill, skirts another wood on the left. This is **Tally Ho Plantation** and the inn looks tantalizingly close; you can even read the name on the sign. But at the corner of the field the path doubles back to the right for a short distance before crossing a shaded footbridge and meeting the A15. Now walk carefully along here to the **Tally Ho! Inn** for your thoroughly deserved lunch.

*Though Aswarby Hall was demolished in 1952, the attractive park still contains two visible curiosities. The first is a pair of Georgian columns, each bearing the boar's head from the Whichcote family crest. The other is a mound near to the road, which is actually the grave of a circus elephant that died near here in 1892. In the church is a memorial to George Bass, the explorer who helped Matthew Flinders to chart the coastline of Australia, but who mysteriously disappeared in 1803, presumed killed and eaten by an Antipodean native.*

⑦ On leaving the inn, continue along the main road, admiring the twin pillars in Aswarby Park and turning left into a narrow open lane in less than 200 yards. In half a mile, where the road bends to the left, branch right onto a signed bridleway. The track crooks left beyond a huge hayrick and then continues for another delightful half mile, passing a wood on your right and soon arriving at a road.

⑧ Continue in the same direction along the side road straight ahead of you (signed for **Aisby** and **Oasby**), turning right in 200 yards when you spot a public footpath sign. The next mile follows a well signed but contorted field-edge path. Eventually, after a short enclosed stretch, a fairly straight half mile leads you to a road in the small farming hamlet of **Culverthorpe**.

⑨ Stroll to the right and at the T-junction a splendid old cast iron signpost ushers you left towards the 'hall only'. Through the grand gates ahead of you, your journey now reaches a climax when the dramatic stone frontage of **Culverthorpe Hall**, flanked by two exquisite ranges of outbuildings, appears along the fenced gravel track through this plush parkland. The track now curves left through the two gates guarding the farm, and goes down the hill to the causeway between the lakes and back to the waterside car park.

*Like a dramatic French chateau, Culverthorpe Hall, with its steeply pitched roof and distinguished north front, first rose up atop the slope overlooking the lake in 1860. It was the seat of the Newton family, to whom Sir Isaac was related, but later passed to the Houblons, whose name is kept alive by the Houblon Arms in Oasby (also passed on the walk). The Newton lineage ended tragically when the only son of Sir Michael Newton was dropped from the parapet of his London home by the family's pet monkey.*

Date walk completed:

# THE SLEA
# NAVIGATION CANAL
# AND EWERBY

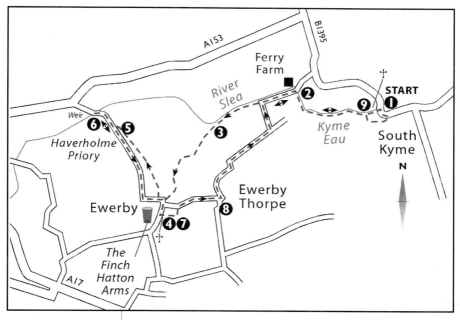

**Distance:**
11½ miles

**Starting point:**
The Hume Arms,
South Kyme.
GR 173495

Maps: OS Landranger 121 (Lincoln) and Landranger 130
(Grantham), or Explorer 261 (Boston)

**How to get there:** *Head south-west towards Sleaford
from Horncastle on the A153. A road signed for South
Kyme (the B1395) branches left, just past North Kyme. In
South Kyme you will be able to park on the roadside –
considerately of course.*

SOUTH KYME TOWER SEEN FROM THE CHURCH

*A*s you follow the disused Slea Navigation canal give rein to your imagination and picture the canal in full swing in the late 1700s, with barges gliding past each other on their journey between Sleaford and the River Witham. Today it is owls and herons that glide in and out of the bulrushes, but this canal still links you to a mighty medieval tower and a crumbling Tudor-style mansion. Across the fields an inn of some distinction, beneath the most perfectly proportioned and uplifting of Gothic spires, beckons you.

Ewerby's Angel Inn became the **Finch Hatton Arms** when the estate owner, Lord Winchilsea, conferred upon it the family name in 1875. The huge inn sign displays the family crest and motto. Set behind lawns, the inn itself is screened by drooping willows and shrubs, and actually looks less like a hostelry than a large Victorian country house. Now grasp the door handles moulded into the shape of two huge Lincoln imps and throw open the doors. Inside, the dark panelling and beamed ceiling shape a number of alcoves and nooks adorned by a fascinating collection of antiques and images of Haverholme Priory. The landlord has been welcoming groups of walkers for many years, and several rambling clubs have made the pub their base. An unusually large range of tempting starters includes escargots and a cheeseboard of hot cheeses. Favourite main courses are turkey, ham, and Stilton pie; and Grimsby haddock or plaice fillet, while the honey and mustard salmon and the duck in plum sauce are also very popular. Add to these a choice of four vegetarian options, traditional roasts on Sundays, and an assortment of sandwiches and snacks for the less hearty eater, and there's something for everyone. Dixon's Major from Wainfleet is one of the ales on offer, along with a guest such as Everards Tiger or Clark's Scrooge's Brew during the festive season.

The Finch Hatton Arms is open for meals every day, serving between 12 noon and 2 pm and again from 6.30 pm to 9.30 pm.

**Telephone:** *01529 460363*
*Apart from the Hume Arms at the start in South Kyme, the Finch Hatton Arms is the only refreshment halt on the walk.*

## The Walk

① Opposite the **Hume Arms** in **South Kyme**, a short lane crosses a narrow bridge on its way to **Low Road**. Here a grassy footpath heads west along the south bank of the **Kyme Eau**, which is an extension of the **River Slea** and part of the **Slea Navigation canal**.

*In 1794 the newly completed Slea Navigation canal finally linked Sleaford with the River Witham near to Tattershall. The large stone portal of the navigation wharf still stands in the town. Though the canal brought industry and wealth to Sleaford, the advent of the railways led to the common tale of decline throughout the second half of the 19th century, and the canal was finally abandoned in 1878. The Slea Navigation Trust has been trying since 1977 to reverse the decline and has already returned much of the canal to a navigable state.*

Past a carved wooden post, this quite enchanting tree-lined segment of the canal towpath leads to a bridge just beyond the medieval tower. Continue along the bank beyond the bridge; the canal is still wide and deep and clear, but the leafy surroundings give way to wide open views of fine steeples on the skyline, with **Heckington** and **Ewerby** prominent. An unexpectedly straight stretch then follows the course of a far more ancient waterway, the Roman **Car Dyke**, and takes you as far as a road bridge at **Ferry Farm**.

② Turn left onto the road here and choose either the easy tarmac surface or the elevated canal bank top, now offering extensive views towards Tattershall Castle, Lincoln Minster, and Boston Stump. At a group of farm buildings called **The Grange**, the road angles away from the canal, but you must continue along the waterside, either on the levee or down on the fieldside track. In less than a mile, just past a pond in a small spinney, the lower track widens and veers away from the canal between open arable fields.

③ Follow this track and, when it bends to the left, cross the bridge over a dyke, and immediately turn right onto a narrower path, keeping the dyke on your right. Go straight ahead now, with Ewerby's handsome church spire always in your sights. Bear to the right at a plank footbridge, and then left, to follow a twisting ditch towards a row of trees ahead. Where the trees start, so also does a track on their left, which upgrades gradually until, as **Field Lane**, it enters the village of **Ewerby**. The market square and stone cross with the church spire soaring behind are now a short walk

THE SLEA NAVIGATION CANAL, HAVERHOLME

in front of you, and across the road is the **Finch Hatton Arms**.

④ Now retrace your steps from the inn but do not re-enter Field Lane, continuing rather along the road you are on for a full mile and a half. Midway, at a belt of woodland, the surrounding landscape becomes a more formal park as you gain your first sight of the gaunt ruins of **Haverholme Priory** on your left.

*The ruins seen are in fact those of the Tudor-style mansion built here in 1830 by the Finch Hattons, many of whom were buried at the church in Ewerby. Of Haverholme Priory, a Gilbertine house founded in 1139, nothing remains.*

⑤ **Keeper's Cottage** on your right is the first of a series of ornate lodges, halls, and gardens, beyond which the road sweeps round to a grandiose stone bridge supporting eight huge stone spheres. This is the furthest extent of the walk and you should take time to explore this wonderful spot. The small car park offers another good view of the priory ruins over the top of two stout square gate piers. The canal below hardly looks navigable here, but just a few yards into the wood a fascinating disused lock (currently undergoing restoration) indicates that it once must have been. Some of the original lock machinery remains on view.

⑥ About turn now to begin the return journey. Do not be lured by a footpath shown on your OS map wending its way towards South Kyme along the opposite canal bank; though delightful initially, it eventually leaves you stranded in dense undergrowth. Retrace your route as far as **Keeper's Cottage**. Just past here, a footpath branches into the field on the left. You will be able to tell instantly whether or not this footpath through crop is in place. If it is, you have a clear and interesting alternative to the outward route; if not, simply continue along **Park Lane** all the way into **Ewerby**. The footpath stays close to the road at first, slowly edging further into the field and eventually crossing a track before plunging along a narrow path through the belt of trees. Then continue over two more fields to an obvious footbridge, and go back onto the road near **Ewerby** via another small bridge.

⑦ Opposite the **Finch Hatton Arms**, leave **Ewerby** along the tiniest of lanes, which leads round the yard of the spectacular spire before striking out across the fenland. Now follows a lengthy and fairly straightforward section of road walking, along which the views remain excellent and progress can be swift. Turn right to rejoin the main road out of **Ewerby** and, passing a curious huge barn of a house dressed in white wooden boarding at **Ewerby Thorpe**, ignore the right turn to **Heckington** and **Howell**.

⑧ The narrow lane ahead twists this way and that at first before taking you all the way back to **The Grange**, followed by the neatly trimmed hedges of **Ferry Farm** in another half mile. Now retrace your earlier footprints along the **Kyme Eau** until you reach the concrete bridge. This time, walk over the bridge and along a fenced lane into a very special setting, silent and eerie, where the ancient nave of a church can be seen on one side and the mighty tower of a medieval castle stands in splendid isolation on the other.

*In South Kyme rows of tall chestnut trees frame the exquisite triangle of tower, church, and hall. All three are set in the same ridged fields where the Augustinian monks of the grand priory here once lived and worked. Remains of dry fishponds and moats can still be found. The four-storey tower now stands alone, all other fragments of the 14th century tower house having been dismantled in the 1700s. The castle is rarely accessible to the public, but the projecting stair turret leading up to the battlements is still clearly visible.*

⑨ Having thoroughly digested this fitting climax to the day's walk, look for a kissing-gate on your right, just past the church gateway; this leads into a paddock and through a gate on the other side you will find yourself back in **South Kyme**, with the **Hume Arms** just around the corner.

*In the 1990s the North Kesteven Arts programme offered commissions to many of the country's finest sculptors, and three of the pieces can be seen on this walk. Simon Todd's* Fox and Pheasant *at the Haverholme bridge over the Slea and his* Kingfisher *next to the same river in South Kyme are two. The third – also in South Kyme – is an elaborate metal arch celebrating the 200th anniversary of the Slea Navigation.*

*Date walk completed:*

# BARROWBY, THE VIKING WAY AND ALLINGTON

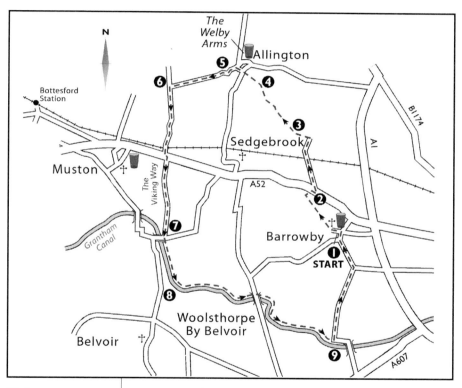

**Distance:**
10¹/₂ miles

**Starting point:**
Barrowby.
GR 880364

**Maps: OS Landranger 130 (Grantham) or Explorer 247 (Grantham)**

**How to get there:** *The village of Barrowby is easily located; set off west from Grantham on the A52 in the direction of Nottingham. As soon as you have crossed the A1, a signed road to the left directs you to Barrowby, a mere half-mile further on, and there is ample roadside parking.*

THE GRANTHAM CANAL, AT DENTON WHARF

*T*his journey through some of the most splendid countryside Lincolnshire has to offer incorporates sections of a charming winding canal towpath and an ancient Bronze Age track, now adopted as part of the Viking Way. Sensational views across the Vale of Belvoir to the serrated silhouette of a hilltop castle are a highlight, and two lovely villages with many original stone houses are explored. There is a price to pay for these rewards, however: the day begins and ends with a very steep hill, and, away from the canal, the going underfoot can be heavy.

The little-visited village of Allington boasts a real gem of a country pub, set proudly on the green, opposite an old market cross in the centre of the village. Although most of Allington's best architecture is of mellow stone, the **Welby Arms** is a neat brick building, covered in creepers and bearing the date 1647 above its porch. In sunny weather the seating on the small lawn at the front is the perfect spot to enjoy a drink and something to eat. Inside, a charming bar area with log fires at each end leads to the rear, where several rooms have been converted into a comfortable restaurant area. The menus are chalked onto blackboards, and the food is all freshly home-made and sounds very tempting. Favourites are Landlord pie, Jim's 'special' fish pie, and Grimsby haddock and chips. If you are looking for something a little more unusual, try the pork schnitzel in Jaeger sauce or the chicken with bacon in creamy Brie sauce. There are excellent steaks, roast beef and Yorkshire pudding on Sundays, and a range of lighter snacks during the week. The dessert menu – if you do still have room – includes sticky toffee pudding. Beers are Taylor's Landlord, John Smith's, and Bass, plus two changing guest beers, such as Spitfire.

Meals are available at the Welby Arms from 12 noon to 2 pm, beginning again in the evening at 6.30 pm. The inn can also provide overnight accommodation.

**Telephone:** *01400 281361*
*The Dirty Duck at Woolsthorpe Bridge also offers fine meals, and there is a pub in Barrowby at the start of the excursion.*

 *The Walk*

① **Barrowby's** centre is well stocked with splendid old stone buildings. If you stand outside the **White Swan** and look over the road, you will see **Church Street** winding past the 19th century reading room and elegant Barrowby Hall, clearly dated 1691. Along here you soon find yourself facing the wooden lychgate of the church; look left to spot a public footpath sign. The path skirts the churchyard and suddenly confronts a quite astonishing prospect: far below, a panorama extends over the vast patchwork plain that is the Trent Valley, and much of the walk before

you is visible from this point. Do not go through the gate ahead of you but go over a stile on your left. Only then bear right to conduct the descent; two fields and two stiles guide you to a clearer track beyond. This gentle grass track soon arrives at a firmer one near to a mound. Turn right here and follow the gravel track to the main road.

② Do not join the road, however, but continue along the inside edge of the field to your right until a footbridge takes you onto the road. Cross with due care, and on the other side join a side road named **Allington Lane**, along which, beyond a level crossing at **Dairy Farm**, the metalled surface gives way to a rougher track and leads to a private access sign barring further progress. Here another attractive hedged lane, to your left, leads you for half a mile to a puzzling junction of dwindling lanes and hedgerows.

③ Your route is straight ahead along a narrow field-edge pathway which follows a hedge on its left. At the end of this path, a stile takes you into a meadow, on the other side of which, through a gate, is a grassy paddock. Next, over a further stile, your way is along a clear path diagonally crossing the two arable fields on your right, although a diversion around the edge of the second field may be required. The new chalet-style development ahead of you is known as **Allington Gardens**, and, inexplicably, the right of way briefly enters the perimeter via a stile and departs by another.

④ Pay close attention now as you approach the village of **Allington**. A narrow wooded path between the development and a water treatment plant leads to a concrete bridge, which you cross before continuing along an even narrower path by the wire fence. Soon a stile brings you into a pasture, and then, over a second stile ahead of you, you find yourself on a track near to a farm. Follow this left and round a corner to arrive at a road; here turn right to stroll into the village of **Allington**, where you will be grateful to discover the **Welby Arms** on the right-hand side of a tapering village green.

*The old stone cross in the centre of Allington is a market cross. Allington was second only to Grantham in the Middle Ages and in 1341 even exceeded Grantham in terms of wool tax payable. The village was part of the estate owned by the Welbys for almost 200 years until its sale in 1944. The poet George Crabbe was rector here between 1790 and 1814.*

⑤ Suitably refreshed, prepare for a more straightforward, if lengthier, return journey. Facing the remains of the cross, at the head of the green turn right into

**THE WELBY ARMS IN ALLINGTON**

**Bottesford Road**, soon passing the Manor House of golden stone, flanked by pairs of ornate Dutch gables dating from 1660. On reaching the village playing field, cross diagonally – assuming no game is taking place, of course – and continue along the lane. Do not be tempted by the footpath shown on your OS map; it leads only to heartache!

⑥ Almost a mile along this lane you arrive at a crossroads, at which you turn left onto a grassy track developing into one of Lincolnshire's lovely wide-verged green lanes. This is an ancient track known as **Sewstern Lane**, as well as being the course of the **Viking Way**.

*Of uncertain origin, Sewstern Lane – also known as The Drift – was probably an important route during the Bronze Age, displaced only when Roman Ermine Street became the preferred route. The distinct absence of settlements and facilities contributed to further decline during the day of the stagecoach, but when turnpikes and tolls were introduced on the main routes, The Drift rose in popularity once more, as a cheap and direct route south for drovers and their animals.*

A further mile brings you over a level crossing to the busy A52. Cross with care and continue along a tarmac lane on the far side. At **Mill Farm**, the lane becomes a track once again and veers into **Shipman's Plantation**; do not deviate from your southerly direction along this lane. (When I did this walk the ruts in the mud at one point, caused by modern farm machinery, were more like the trenches of a battlefield than a public right of way.) However, a quite magnificent view unfurls before you of the wooded hills, with the ducal towers and turrets of **Belvoir Castle** as their crown.

*This is the fourth castle to stand on this site, which dominates the Vale of Belvoir. The first was built by Robert de Todeni, standard bearer to William the Conqueror. Despite its appearance, the present building dates only to about 1800 and was erected by the Duke of Rutland as a mock medieval castle. It is in truth a stately mansion housing a wealth of fine paintings, furniture, and sculpture, as well as the museum of the Queen's Royal Lancers.*

⑦ At a junction with a quiet lane, cross it and stroll up the firm track ahead of you. This soon joins the bed of a disused railway behind a narrow belt of trees, but far more interesting is to cut through to the grassy canal towpath and begin to absorb the delights of the

**Grantham Canal**. Quite simply, you now follow this most beautiful of canals for almost 3 miles; the path surface upgrades to gravel at **Woolsthorpe Bridge**, close to a popular inn named the **Rutland Arms**, but known locally as the Dirty Duck.

⑧ Beyond two fascinating sets of lock gates, splendid views unfurl through tall trees that arch over the canal. Allow your imagination to stretch back two hundred years to the days when boats and barges plied back and forth along this waterway, in its setting of woods and pastures, with sumptuous **Belvoir** and **Harlaxton Manor** nearby. Today, swans, herons, and moorhens are the canal's principal patrons, and the idyllic picture is completed by numerous low, ivy-clad bridges; this really is all that is finest about the English countryside.

*In 1797 the opening of the Grantham Canal drastically reduced freight costs between Grantham and the Trent at Nottingham. Grain and groceries were unloaded at Nottingham and the barges reloaded with coke, lime, and coal for the return journey. The burgeoning railway network sent the canal into decline from 1851 onwards, but in 1879 the first of many iron ore mines in the area was opened, heralding an upturn in trade. However, only four years after this, the canal was rendered virtually redundant when a branch line linking the main line with the mines at Woolsthorpe, Denton, and Harlaxton was laid. It is the remains of this railway that can be seen along the walk near to Woolsthorpe Bridge.*

⑨ The route now leaves the towpath by a ramp up to a road, which climbs steeply up the hillside to the left, dipping briefly before continuing uphill towards **Barrowby**. Go straight ahead now, through the newer part of the village; the old stone centre of **Barrowby** – your journey's end – is just half a mile in front of you.

*Date walk completed:*

# WELLINGORE, COLEBY AND NAVENBY

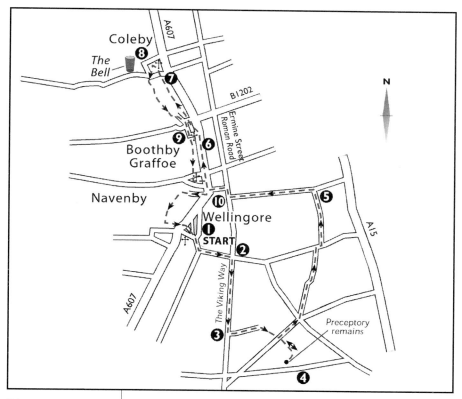

**Distance:**
11 miles

**Starting point:**
*High Street,*
*Wellingore.*
*GR 984566*

**Maps: OS Landranger 121 (Lincoln) or Explorer 272 (Lincoln)**

**How to get there:** *Wellingore, 9 miles south of Lincoln and 16 miles north of Grantham, is one of many villages strung along the A607. You should have no trouble finding a parking spot in the village; otherwise locate the Memorial Hall car park, signed to the west of the A607.*

THE WELLHEAD, COLEBY

*T*his walk consists of two very distinct sections. The first part of the day is a lengthy but level trek across the heathland south of Lincoln to discover the fascinating remnants of a monastery founded by the Knights Templar. The rest of the day is spent along the Viking Way, visiting a chain of attractive villages built entirely in stone and precariously situated at the top of the Lincoln Cliff, overlooking the Brant Valley. An inn of some distinction is hidden at the end of a lane in one of these villages, a suitable reward for your efforts.

Hidden at the end of a twisting lane behind Coleby's crocketed spire, is **The Bell**. To attract custom, it has to rely entirely on its reputation – there is positively no passing trade here. It is not until you enter that you realize what a special place this is. The menus are many and varied, with some choices listed on boards around the bar areas. All the food is of the highest quality, and meals are served with fresh home-made bread. Of particular interest are the six

Spanish-style tapas, and a wide choice of hot and cold club sandwiches. On Sundays, roast lunches are added to the menu – they're very popular and deservedly so. Vegetarians might select the tomato, mushroom, and couscous gateau or the asparagus and artichoke frittata. The beers are well kept. As well as Black Sheep from Masham, you will always find a guest beer, such as Jennings Cumberland Ale.

The Bell serves meals between 11.30 am and 2.30 pm and between 5.30 pm and 9 pm from Monday to Saturday. On Sundays, meals are available from 12 noon to 8 pm.

**Telephone:** *01522 810240*
*Other inns serving food can be found in Wellingore and Navenby; Navenby also has a range of shops to cater for your needs.*

## The Walk

① From the narrow **High Street** in **Wellingore**, head away from the main A607 to unite with the road leading in from the church and Wellingore Hall. **Hall Street** now leads you to **Pottergate Road**; turn right here to leave the village, and then left at the next side road, signed to **Temple Bruer**.

② Half a mile along this road turn right into **Holly Lane**, which is not only part of the **Viking Way** but also on the course of **Roman Ermine Street**, to which it owes its die-straight direction.

*Along Holly Lane, concrete pillboxes indicate the former site of RAF Wellingore on the right, and a mounted section of a tail*

*fin next to an information plaque confirms this.*

③ In a mile, the road swings to the left and assumes a more intimate feel as hedges of holly and hawthorn close in. Past **Griffin's Farm**, the tarmac gives way to an open chalky track between fields under cultivation, followed by an exhilarating trek across the windy heathland. Bearing right at a three-way junction along the way, you soon find yourself at **Temple Farm**, and, round the first corner, the startling tower of **Temple Bruer** preceptory comes into view.

*The Knights Templar was an order of soldier monks formed in 1118, following the first crusade to the Holy Lands. The Knights built a chain of preceptories throughout Europe to shelter pilgrims bound for Jerusalem. Part cathedral, part castle, the preceptories also served as farms, the revenue from wool and agriculture helping to finance the order's military activities overseas. The core of the preceptory was a large circular nave – a feature unique to Templar churches – linked to twin square towers. In the 1530s the dissolution of the monasteries led to the monastery being dismantled, and one of the towers is all that now remains of this mighty house. But this is still an evocative spot to visit, set in a neat lawn and surrounded by farm buildings, probably built of stones from the preceptory.*

④ Having surveyed this hidden gem, retrace your steps to the three-way junction along the track, turning right here onto a metalled lane. In less than half a mile, you come to a grand meeting of ways at a lonely little roadside church, designed by James Fowler in 1874. Pass to the right of the church to embark upon a fairly lengthy hike along typical Lincolnshire green lanes. **New England Lane** guides you for more than a mile to **Gorse Hill Lane**; here walk to the right for a few yards, and then turn left into **Gorse Lane**. The hedges and trees along these lanes offer welcome shelter after the exposed open heath, and

**THE BELL AT COLEBY**

**Gorse Lane**, guarded on one side by a large wood, has an even more enclosed feel.

⑤ This lane has almost dwindled to a single path by the time it reaches the road crossing **Navenby Heath**. Turn left onto this road and continue for another full mile until you find yourself back at **Ermine Street** near **Navenby**. Head right; then take the next road on the left, **Chapel Lane**, venturing briefly into the field known as The Open Space on the corner you have just rounded. On arriving at the main road in **Navenby**, walk through the centre of the village to the right.

⑥ Soon after leaving the last buildings of **Navenby**, the church tower of the next village, **Boothby Graffoe**, becomes your goal. On your first visit, however, do not turn into the village but cross a new stile on your left, just yards further along the main road. Now count the stiles. A tiny copse (1) is followed by a meadow containing a railway carriage employed as a cattle shelter (2), then another copse (3), a donkey paddock (4). Cross over a driveway (5) and go along a narrow path to a road (6). Beyond this, take an even narrower passage (7), another paddock (8) and finally go onto a farm track (9!). Straight ahead of you, a gate leads from the small farmyard into a huge cornfield, through which an obvious

path targets a break in the hedgerow ahead. From here a good track goes past a shallow disused quarry and onto **Dovecote Lane** above **Coleby**.

⑦ **Coleby** is perhaps the finest of this string of handsome stone-built villages. To best enjoy it, turn left and saunter down the hill to a green, with the **Tempest Arms** opposite you. Turn right into **Blind Lane**, and pass another green featuring twin stone well-heads of the pepperpot variety. Turn left into **Rectory Lane** at the T-junction, right at the crossroads near the church, and, as you are about to give up hope of finding much along this narrowing lane, spot a beckoning inn on your left – **The Bell**.

⑧ From the pub, continue along **Far Lane**; in just a few yards, a kissing-gate takes you instantly into countryside once again – not the wild expanses of the heath, but a delightful grassy terrace along the **Lincoln Cliff**, overlooking the fertile valleys of the rivers Witham and Brant, and the Trent beyond. The first section takes you left through three fields. A third stile returns you alongside the **Tempest Arms** to the green in **Coleby**. Outside the pub look to your right to locate a signed public footpath, which is extremely narrow at first, given that you are now on the **Viking Way**. The way along the cliff is now clear, continuing over one stile after another, until one takes you into a neat paddock on your left, which you cross diagonally and exit by a stable. Now in **Far End**, follow the lane into **Boothby Graffoe's Main Street**, savouring this most attractive part of the village.

⑨ As **Main Street** turns to climb back up to the church, a track running alongside **Hillside Cottage** on your right winds back towards the terrace on the slope with which you have become familiar. As you pass a wood on your left, you should be able to spot the tower of Somerton Castle two miles across the valley.

*Somerton was developed by the Bishop of Durham as a castle in quadrangular form, with four circular corner towers, each 30 feet in diameter. Today only one of the towers remains complete, adjoining a large farm, while the bases of two of the other towers still stand in the farmyard.*

Eventually the path negotiates a dog-leg on the left and arrives at a road in **Navenby**. Turn left and look for a passageway on your right,

called **Cat Walk**, which guides you through to the church. Turn left along **Church Lane** and head into the hub of the village for the second time.

⑩ Having followed the main road to the right for a few hundred yards, you will espy **Clint's Lane** on your right, at the end of which a narrow field-edge path curves around **Clint's Farm**. When you reach a high hedge, be sure to turn and follow the path to the right; from here one of the journey's best views can be enjoyed, embracing the church above the rooftops of **Navenby**, and the villages perched on the limestone scarp along which you have just walked. At a small wood, look for a stile on your left, over which the final part of the upland terrace is joined. The clear path soon takes you left into an overgrown meadow, and on the far side a kissing-gate leads to the **Wellingore Memorial Hall**. Look for **Memorial Hall Drive** on the right, guiding you out of the car park, and turn left when this reaches **West Street**. Now return to the main road in the village of **Wellingore**.

*Date walk completed:*

# LINCOLN HEATH AND THE CAR DYKE

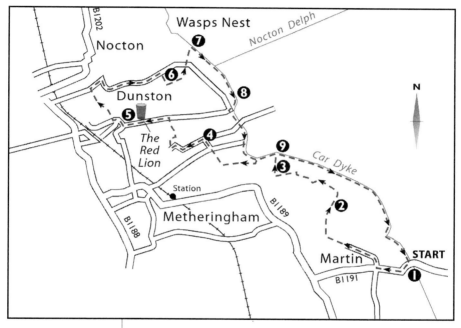

**Distance:**
11½ miles

**Starting point:**
*Martin.*
*GR 128601*

**Maps: OS Landranger 121 (Lincoln), or Explorer 261 (Boston)
Explorer 272 (Lincoln), and Explorer 273 (Lincolnshire Wolds
South)**

**How to get there:** *Take the B1191 west from Woodhall
Spa and in 5 miles you will reach Martin. The best place to
park is just before the road climbs into the village itself,
where a broad road on the left runs alongside the
Car Dyke.*

THE ATTRACTIVE RED LION PUB AT DUNSTON

*W*here the wide stretches of fen around the River Witham meet the gently wooded slopes rising to the heathland in the west, runs an intriguing watercourse, once believed to be a Roman canal, and now the most peaceful and idyllic of countryside trails. Your route will follow the tree-lined Car Dyke for several miles, but not before you have explored the heath itself, where unspoilt villages of warm stone buildings contrast with the eerie deserted runways of a Second World War airfield. Footpaths throughout the area are well indicated by yellow waymarkers. Look out too for a number of carved wooden sculptures commissioned and installed to enhance this fine landscape.

Striding towards Dunston's **Red Lion** you allow your spirits to rise. Ivy creeps up the long low stone walls of this most handsome of village inns to the bright pantiles above. Borders and baskets of flowers create a blaze of colour in the summer, while in colder weather the inn appears warm and welcoming and a warren of delightful rooms offers you a choice of places to settle. There are exposed stone walls in the low intimate dining room, a real log fire in the smaller lounge, inglenooks and wooden beamed ceilings too – no wonder the place always seems busy. Local folk, tourists, and travellers converge here to create a lively atmosphere and test the inn's reputation. A daily specials board supplements the menu, and at lunchtimes on Sunday traditional roasts can also be ordered. Delicious steaks are a speciality and the home-made steak pie is popular. You might choose the salmon fillet with a mustard and herb crust, while the ravenous may favour the 'generous gammon steak'! Lighter meals, such as jacket potatoes, baps and burgers, are on offer, as well as good options for vegetarians: spinach and marscapone lasagne or mushroom and nut fettuccine. Eye-catching desserts, such as chocolate and brandy truffle torte, will test the discipline of the dedicated walker, as will the guest ale (for example, Bombardier) which always accompanies the permanent beers: Tetley, Bass, and Caffreys.

The Red Lion observes normal serving hours, with meals available from 12 noon to 2 pm (11.30 am to 2 pm on Saturdays and Sundays). Evening meals begin at about 7 pm, and you should note that, apart from at the starting point in Martin, no other shops or inns will be found along the route.

**Telephone:** *01526 322227*

 *The Walk*

① From the parking area next to the **Car Dyke**, make your way up the hill into **Martin**. Of particular interest is The Stables, a gallery selling superior ceramics and paintings. Just past the church, turn right into **Linwood Road**, being sure to branch left into **North Moor Lane**, a short distance along here. By the time you pass a derelict farm on your left, the route has downgraded to a narrow path along the edge of a field. When you reach a gravel track, turn left, and then turn right when you gain a metalled surface once more. You are now walking along one of the runways of Metheringham's former RAF base; just behind you is a memorial, and beyond that is the visitor centre.

*In 1942, an area of some 650 acres of wood and farmland was cleared, and, less than a year later, Metheringham Airfield was operational. Of the countless Lancaster bombers of 106 Squadron that took off from here bound for targets in Germany – mainly Berlin – 57 never returned. At its peak, more than 2,000 personnel were in service at*

*Metheringham, and the roles of these people, the aircraft, and the airfield are commemorated in an exhibition at the Metheringham Airfield visitor centre nearby.*

② Straight over the next road, your route continues past a red bar gate and sweeps round a broad left-hand curve. At the end of the next straight, turn right onto a grassy track when you spot a yellow waymarker. Now target a narrow fenced path running beneath the fir trees that line **Blackthorn Holt's** right-hand border. Turn right when you arrive at a good farm track, and, around a sharp bend to the left, turn right at the next junction to pass spruce, brick **Metheringham Barff Farm**.

③ Striding down the hill, turn left just before the bridge, and follow the shaded **Car Dyke**. When the waterway steers to the right, your path branches clearly to the left, but a less conspicuous track leading to the right a few yards past here must not be missed; a footbridge crossing a forded stream will confirm your navigational skills. When this track reaches a field corner, do not follow the field edge to the right, but step through an obvious gap in the trees and continue along a narrower path on the other side. Having angled to the right, the route now develops into a hedged green lane and maintains the same direction when it joins a road.

④ At a sign for **Prior Lane**, turn left onto a side road, and, reaching a

'AN EXCHANGE OF ELEMENTS', THE CAR DYKE, MARTIN

row of conifer trees at the next bend, continue straight ahead onto a stony farmtrack. Beyond a double bend, a clear yellow arrow directs you right, onto a grassy footpath, which twists this way and that before taking you through a farmyard and onto **Dunston Fen Lane**. Turn left here and stroll into the village of **Dunston** itself. A clear stream comes alongside as you enter the village, bridged in several places and bisecting the pretty green. This is an excellent spot to linger, and a few steps to your right is the **Red Lion**.

*The Dunston Pillar rises from the heathlands three miles west of here. It was erected as a land lighthouse to guide travellers across these notorious parts, but the lantern at its summit was later replaced by a 14 feet high statue of George III, famously insane, and it is this image that inspired Simon Todd's (see also Walk 7) sculpture in the centre of Dunston. The grave of John Wilson, the mason who mounted the King's statue on top of the pillar, can be found at Harmston, bearing the epitaph:*

> *He who erected the noble King*
> *Is here now laid by Death's*
> *sharp sting.*

⑤ From the **Red Lion** continue west along the winding lane, and turn right when you see **Back Lane**.

Along here, a narrow gap just past the school opens onto a hedge-lined footpath leading to **Nocton**. (An exploration of this fine stone-built village will be fully rewarded.) The route proper, however, turns right just before the village to follow a row of oak trees flanking the village cricket pitch. The lane you are now on leads through a superior parkscape and past a series of interesting features, beginning with **Nocton church**, and also including a stone lodge, a small lake, and a water tower.

⑥ A mile along here, at a sign reading 'road used as a public footpath', turn right to briefly re-enter wooded surroundings; then turn left onto a signed bridleway which passes a conspicuous green barn. At the end of an enclosed section, the bridleway unites with a concrete track guiding you down the hill to **Wasps' Nest**, as you enjoy the day's best views over the fenland below you, the wide level valley of the **River Witham**.

⑦ **Wasps' Nest**, the site of the 12th century **Nocton Priory**, is a quite exquisitely situated farming hamlet on the course of the **Car Dyke**, which will now accompany you for your entire return journey. Turn right through the farm gate to embark upon the first section of the walk along the dyke, between deep woods rising on the far bank and the vast fens, silent and atmospheric. This really is walking at its most perfect.

*Dr William Stukeley, the 18th century historian, invented the romantic notion of grain barges plying back and forth along the Car Dyke to feed the Roman armies in the north. It is now believed that it was actually part of an ingenious drainage system, known as a ringvart, which allowed water to flow in both directions and enabled the reclamation and cultivation of the adjacent fens. Beside this trail the dyke is a veritable arboretum, where the small-leaved lime, a native of central Lincolnshire, is among the trees that can be found.*

⑧ At a picnic area, join the incoming road and follow it around the wood, turning left at a roadsign for **Metheringham Fen**. At the T-junction turn right (signed **Metheringham**), locate and negotiate a stile on your left, and exit the field you are in via another stile. Now along a narrow sheep pasture, descend gradually towards the water running alongside, and, clearing the next stile, walk beside the **Car Dyke** into a narrow belt of woodland. Along this short straight section, the channel appears almost ornamental, and you cross by means of the earth bank. Beyond a brief

open stretch of pathway the waterway winds into a quite idyllic wooded tract – you will recognize your outward route on the opposite bank. On reaching the brick bridge for the second time, do not cross and ascend to **Metheringham Barff Farm**, but continue along the waterside, now on a firm concrete farmtrack.

⑨ Progress now is swift and certain, and for a mile and a half this track continues unhindered past a series of sturdy brick farmhouses. Do not deviate, even when roads from left and right join you, and, when the road angles away from the water at a farm, stay true to the watercourse, following a gravel track past **Tramp's Cottage** to a stile. Beyond here the bank is once again grassy underfoot and becomes more open past an oak sculpture entitled *An Exchange of Elements*. Two stiles lead you over a lane at **Linwood Hall Farm** before the **Car Dyke** crooks sharply to the left in the next field. Remain on the raised bank around this bend; one stile later, the path meets a road coming in over the fen. Along this road, the end of your journey below the village of **Martin** is just yards ahead of you – time for a souvenir from The Stables?

*Date walk completed:*

# WOODHALL SPA, THE HORNCASTLE CANAL AND KIRKBY ON BAIN

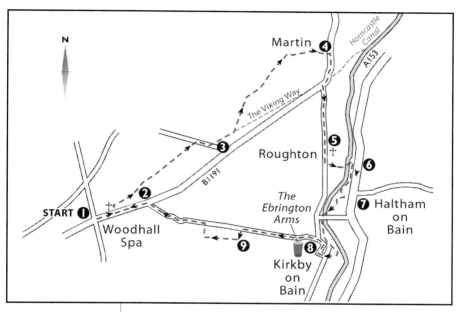

**Distance:**
9¹/₂ miles

**Starting point:**
Woodhall Spa.
GR 193631

Maps: OS Landranger 122 (Skegness) or Explorer 273
(Lincolnshire Wolds South)

**How to get there:** *Woodhall Spa is easily located 6 miles south-west of Horncastle, on the B1191, and 4 miles north-west of Coningsby, on the B1192. Park either on the roadside in the town centre or in Jubilee Park, along Stixwould Road.*

THE PATH THROUGH OSTLERS' PLANTATION

Sir John Betjeman labelled Woodhall Spa 'that most Bournemouth-like settlement in the middle of Lincolnshire'. It was once a spa resort and is currently the home of the National Golf Centre. Woodhall has a wealth of history to offer, and it is a fascinating little town to explore before setting out on this varied trail. Along the way the bed of an old railtrack, a former canal towpath, and a trip through a forest linked to Woodhall's birth are embraced. Dense woods and wide open fields are traversed, and there is a halt at a shaded inn in one of the villages along the canal towpath.

**The Ebrington Arms** in Kirkby on Bain is the most wonderfully sited country inn, shaded by an enormous weeping willow and overlooking a junction of narrow byroads. The tiny walled forecourt is a fine spot from which to take in these peaceful surroundings, while behind the inn runs the canal, where a mill, a wharf, and a lock can still be seen. There is a casual, friendly atmosphere inside the pub, enhanced by low oak beams covered in several hundred beer mats, a real log fire, and a good selection of bar table-top games. The fare, all home-made, plentiful and delicious, consists mainly of favourites such as steak and ale pie – the large square plated variety – and battered cod and chips. Locally sourced ingredients are favourites; the Sausthorpe Lincoln sausage ring is popular, and Saxelbye Stilton is used for the vegetarian puff-pastry tart. Traditional roast lunches replace the usual menu on Sundays, when, please note, chips are available to children only! Abbot Ale and Bateman's XB are among the ales always on offer, plus a guest such as Tetley Imperial or Adnams.

Meals can be ordered at the Ebrington between 12 noon and 2 pm at lunchtimes and from 7 pm to 9 pm in the evenings (6.30 pm on Fridays and Saturdays). No food is available on Sunday evenings, and the inn is closed on Mondays except Bank Holidays.

**Telephone:** *01526 354560*
*Along the route the Marmion Arms in Haltham also provides excellent meals, and there is a wide choice of venues to eat and drink at in Woodhall Spa.*

 *The Walk*

① Beginning at the Dambusters' Memorial in **Woodhall's Eagle Square**, head briefly along **The Broadway** before forking left into **Spa Road**, which leads you away from the Edwardian arcades into the pine woods behind. Where the road angles left towards the spa and the Kinema in the Woods, your route is straight ahead along **Manor Road**. Now following one of the finest stretches of the **Viking Way**, you soon pass a complex of buildings, old and new, serving the courses radiating from Woodhall's **National Golf Centre**.

② Rather than curve towards this complex, continue in your original direction along a lesser track, which now passes through the attractive surroundings of the courses themselves. Please remain courteous to the players on these links, as well as alert to low-flying golf balls threatening your own well-being. Via fairways, footbridges, and woodland paths lined with bright rhododendrons, this privileged pathway finally arrives at a road. Turn right onto the road for about 400 yards, and then turn left when you meet the old bed of the railway to **Horncastle**.

③ Still surrounded by deep woods, seek a public bridleway sign on your left, opposite a white house on the right. This bridleway disappears into even more dense woods, but the twisting path is easy to follow. Now on the walk's most adventurous section, you emerge into sunlight after half a mile to follow an arable field-edge path, but you are plunged back into the greenery where **Whitehall Wood** and **Thornton Wood** come alongside each other. Leaving the woods, the bridleway continues as a broad grassy swathe between arable fields. When this luxuriant track ends abruptly, turn right to pursue a narrow field path, which develops to a good track once more as it encounters three consecutive kissing-gates on its way into the still, farming hamlet of **Martin**, comprising a hall, an ancient little church, a farm, and a couple of houses – and no more.

④ Carry on through Martin's central courtyard to a road, onto which you turn right and walk as far as a side road, which is signed for **Roughton** on the left, just beyond a railway bridge. Fine views across the **Bain Valley** now accompany you along this lane until you enter the compact village of **Roughton**, noteworthy for its thatched white cottages and a couple of elegant brick halls.

⑤ Through the village and down the hill, seek a footpath sign and stile on your left. The path crosses a meadow and a track on its way to a narrow railed footbridge; a few yards past here, you clear a stile to enter the next meadow. Now a modest footbridge crosses the rather sullen trickle of the **Old River Bain** before an entirely grander bridge takes you over the **Horncastle Canal**.

*Completed in 1802, the Horncastle Canal linked the town with Tattershall and the River Witham in the south. It had eleven locks in eleven miles and could carry boats of up to 50 tons. Though further boosted by the opening of a railway along the north bank of the Witham, it was another rail link, between Horncastle and Kirkstead, that later led to the decline of the canal. The last recorded cargo was in 1878, when a barge carrying 31 tons of*

THE EBRINGTON ARMS AT KIRKBY ON BAIN

*guano made the journey from Boston to Horncastle.*

⑥ Turn right and stroll alongside the canal until the clear meadow path veers away from the water towards the perimeter fence of the nearby gardens, which it hugs as far as a gateway just before a large circular cattle trough. Go through the gateway and over the next grassy field to find yourself in the village of **Haltham-on-Bain**, which is well worth exploring to your left as far as the fascinating hidden church and the **Marmion Arms**, a handsome thatched and half-timbered building.

*Now in the care of the Redundant Churches Fund, St Benedict's in Haltham holds treasures inside and out. The colossal east window contains flowing stone tracery worthy of the giants in the south of the county, and the interior escaped the worst of the Victorian restoration programme. Important wooden furnishings include medieval pews, a three-decker pulpit, and family box pews, one of which belonged to the Dymokes, the hereditary Champions of England.*

⑦ Now return along the length of **West Lane**, turning left just before you reach a new housing area, and crossing a stile to the right of the final house to enter a pasture. (I dismissed the 'beware of the bull'

sign in rather blasé fashion, but some of those horns did look very long! However, I discovered that the wide stares were of curiosity not ferocity as I hurried across the field.) Exit over a stile by a group of bushes, and, slanting across the next field, target the white rails of **Red Mill Bridge**. Cross the road via two stiles, and continue along the pleasant levee, with the canal once more on your right. Approaching a mill building, you find your progress barred by a fence, but your route simply follows the fence to the left, crosses two stiles, and beyond a tangled patch of undergrowth rejoins the towpath. On the far bank you will soon see a small church; cross the canal by the gated footbridge here, and, now in **Kirkby-on-Bain**, walk through the pine-shaded churchyard to the lane. At the turning circle, a footpath sign shepherds you to the right, and along here you pass behind the old school, cross another lane, and continue along a very confined footpath. On emerging at a lane, head right through a jumble of old houses lining Kirkby's main street, soon to see the willows draping over the bright white frontage of the welcoming **Ebrington Arms**.

⑧ If you stand by the willow in the inn grounds, you can see **Moor Lane** (signed **Woodhall Spa**) climbing the hill opposite you. It is a quiet lane, and the lack of a footpath means that some alertness is required. For about a mile, this lane leads you through the distinctive heathland of **Kirkby Moor**. Far removed from the heavy clays of the **Bain Valley**, the sandy soil here supports birch and pine, gorse and bracken. Rabbit burrows and squirrels are everywhere, and evidence of badgers can be seen. When you reach a wood on your left, ignore the first entrance at a gate and cattle-grid, and at the next entrance take the narrow path through the bracken into **Ostler's Plantation**.

⑨ At a group of particularly tall pines, take the path on your right, leading alternately through open heathland and belts of towering evergreens – if it's cones you collect, this is the place for you! When you arrive at a car park, turn to the right to leave Ostler's Plantation, and then follow the road to the left for almost a mile. Through a pretty residential area, still dominated by trees all around, you eventually arrive at **The Broadway**, with **Eagle Square** a short distance to the left.

*Of particular interest along the way are the imposing Golf Hotel, which is an ornate black and white construction rivalling nearby Petwood, and the tiny Cottage Museum housing the tourist information centre.*

*John Parkinson's failed dream – to build a city, plant a forest, and sink a mine – led to Woodhall's rise to prosperity. When he was declared bankrupt in 1826, the water flooding his mineshaft was discovered to have curative properties, and the town expanded quickly around the beneficial mineral waters of its new spa. His forests, meanwhile, had to be sold, and Ostler's Plantation is all that remains.*

*In the town centre's Royal Square, look for a memorial in the shape of a dam. In 1943, Woodhall's Petwood Hotel became the officer's mess of 617 Squadron – the 'Dambusters'. Their finest hour came with the successful attack, led by Wing Commander Guy Gibson VC, on six dams in the Ruhr, Germany's industrial heartland.*

*Date walk completed:*

# NETTLEHAM, DUNHOLME, SCOTHERN AND SUDBROOKE PARK

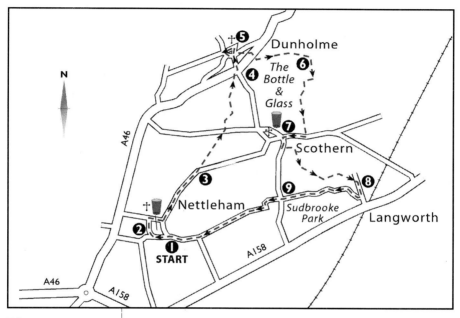

**Distance:**
9 miles

**Starting point:**
Nettleham.
GR 008753

**Maps: OS Landranger 121 (Lincoln) or Explorer 272 (Lincoln)**

**How to get there:** *Nettleham is 4 miles north-east of Lincoln. Two signed roads lead into the village from the A46, as do two from the parallel A158. There is parking around the green in the village centre and in the nearby streets.*

THE BECK AT NETTLEHAM

*T*here can be few better places to seek peace and solitude than the open fields to the north-east of Lincoln and few better ways of enjoying their solace than on a lengthy ramble around the region, which is mainly arable and nowhere hilly. Three separate rivers flow through three villages on their journeys to Barlings Eau, crossed here by a bridge and there by a ford. We start in one of these villages, where a variety of species of ducks wander in and out of the stream by the shaded churchyard, and midway stop to enjoy a meal in a typical Lincolnshire country inn in another.

**The Bottle and Glass** certainly deserves its prime position at the crossroads in Scothern, where the narrow beck is channelled alongside the pub garden before disappearing under the forecourt. Painted neatly in cream, with a steep pantile roof and an arched porchway, the inn has a most charming appearance. Real fires and beams, a mind-boggling collection of pewter tankards, and two windows with stained glass insets of the bottle and glass motif lend charm to the interior too, and the atmosphere is friendly and chatty. A rather special restaurant named Germain's (the saint to whom the nearby church is dedicated) has also been opened, but you will probably elect to eat in the bar. A number of menus operate so there is something for everyone here – from the snack menu offering delicious fillings in Starbuck's bread rolls (the family baker in Market Rasen, not the national chain of cafés) to the specials menu, on which the most popular dishes will be found, such as home-made pies. Finally there is the restaurant menu for those seeking something a bit special – maybe a steak from Phipp's at Mareham or beer-battered Grimsby cod. On Sundays a roast carvery is added to the choices (booking is advisable), but on Sundays in the quiet season only the carvery is available. Timothy Taylor's Landlord is one of the beers offered, along with John Smith's and Bass.

Bar meals are available from 12 noon to 2 pm and from 5 pm to 7 pm, at which time the restaurant menu takes over, although you can dine in the bar from that menu.

**Telephone:** *01673 862231*
*Elsewhere on the walk there are several busy inns and shops in Nettleham, as well as a small pub in Dunholme.*

 *The Walk*

① From **Nettleham's** green, fringed by cheerful stone houses and inns, start the day with a real treat. Head along **Church Street** to All Saints' church. Do not cross **Jubilee Bridge**, however, but turn right onto the chestnut-shaded path alongside **Nettleham Beck**. In the churchyard on your right stands the gravestone of a 19 year old post-boy, gruesomely murdered in 1732 by the Hallam brothers, while ducks waddling out of the water on the left will demand a toll before you

are allowed to pass. The beckside path passes pleasant stone houses on both sides and a series of bridges before reaching a ford next to an old converted watermill; there were once seven in the village.

② Turn right and ascend **Green Lane**, a sometimes muddy bridleway that leads to **Deepdale Lane**; turn right again here and then left at the T-junction, where a National Cycle Network sign can be seen. Follow **Scothern Lane** out of the village, and in less than a mile, now in open countryside, spot the public footpath sign on your left at **Skelton Corner**.

③ Go through two gates and over a stile on your right; you are now in a sheep pasture and you follow the perimeter hedge. Climb over the next stile. Where the field edge veers off to the right, your pathway heads half-left across the arable field, targeting a railed footbridge over **Scothern Beck**. The path slants still across these fields, crosses a road, and continues on the other side as far as the next footbridge and a farmtrack just past that. Follow the track to the left until it ends at a broken hedge. Through this hedge, resume your diagonal direction on the clear path through the field. At the only boundary along this stretch, the right of way shuffles to the right for a few yards before resuming its original direction

to its terminus at a busy junction.

④ Cross the **Dunholme** bypass with care, and stroll into the centre of this attractive village. At the former main road, turn left, and at the shops, turn right into **Ryland Road**. Look to your right for **Watery Lane**, along which you will find a ford over **Dunholme Beck**. At this point you join the lovely shaded streamside path on your right, passing a pub and finally reaching a bridge at **St Chad's church**, viewed through a screen of majestic beech trees.

*Dunholme has been a peaceful backwater since it was bypassed by the new road. The green adjacent to the church is its prettiest spot; here, where*

**DUNHOLME VILLAGE**

*Dunholme Beck is crossed by a footbridge, is a stone well basin of 1893 and an impressive memorial. Inside the sturdy church, look for two 14th century windows in the south aisle, where stone coffin lids carved with crosses have been used as lintels. Another great rarity from the same century, a beautifully decorated leather chalice case, is also displayed.*

⑤ Beyond the lofty war memorial on the other side of the green, you will spot **Ashing Lane**; follow this out of the village, cross the bypass once more, and continue along the lane for a further half-mile, passing **Ashlin Farm** on the way. Now on a rougher track, look for a footpath sign on your right when **Ashing Lane** becomes enclosed by tall trees.

⑥ This field-edge path passes a rather sparse plantation, follows the hedge to the right, and in 200 yards moves into the field on the left via a stile and a footbridge. Now a broad pathway guides you across the next two fields to pass a barricade, which we will kindly call a display of bygone agricultural machinery. Nevertheless, the route improves from this point. A grassy lane initially, **Northing Lane** upgrades as it passes a series of farms to enter the village of **Scothern**. Turn right and walk into the village, where the **Bottle and Glass** commands a prime central position.

⑦ **Sudbrooke Road** now leads you behind the **Bottle and Glass** as far as a bend where a signed footpath diverts you to the left. This short path crosses a road before reaching a stile overlooking open fields once more. Diagonally cross the first field and go over the stile at the gap in the hedge; now follow the hedge to the right until your path improves to a firm track. The track passes the mechanical nodding donkeys of an oil depot before twisting and turning to arrive at the pleasant fields of the **Sudbrooke estate**, ranks of tall trees fringing the horizon in all directions. When further progress is barred by a no entry sign, a diagonal path across the field on your left leads you to a group of mainly wooden farm buildings, where the track is rejoined. When another track crosses yours, your pathway slants across the next field on your right, beyond which the track is regained, now as a tarmac lane.

⑧ Stay on this lane as it curves to the right. At a junction next to a bridge, turn to the right, ensuring that a dense wood is on your left. Now follow this charming route through ever deepening woodland, into the heart of **Sudbrooke Park**, making sure to branch left onto a lesser track just before more nodding donkeys. Eventually you find yourself in a courtyard bounded by a farm and several private houses. Do not deviate from your westerly direction. Cross the beck and enter **West Drive**, continuing straight ahead when this bends to the left, and finally arriving at the road to **Scothern**.

*Sudbrooke Holme has gone. The mansion built for the Ellison family in the 18th century was pulled down in 1951, and only two lodges and stone gate piers at the main entrance on the Wragby road now remain. In Sudbrooke, if you were to follow West Drive all the way to the road, you would come across an enormous Jurassic sandstone boulder. Scratched, smoothed, and polished by the massive ice sheet carrying it down from the Wolds 300,000 years ago, it is now displayed as the village's Millennium Stone.*

⑨ Turn right onto this road; then almost immediately turn left into **Church Lane** and go through the tiny hamlet of **Sudbrooke**. Now stride out along this open road for a full mile, enjoying a fine view of Lincoln Cathedral ahead of you. On re-entering **Nettleham**, turn right at the T-junction into **Sudbrooke Lane**, and a little further on turn right again into **Vicarage Lane**; a few yards on, you will reach the green in **Nettleham** once more.

*Though expanding uncontrollably as a commuter village, the core of old Nettleham remains unspoilt, with stone buildings dating from the 16th century onwards lining the streets. The church is of some architectural distinction. It was built mainly in the 1300s in the Early English style, but was extensively remodelled by the Victorians. A fire in 1969 led to further renovation of the chancel. Close to the route are the earthworks where once stood the Bishop of Lincoln's palace, first built as Nettleham Manor in 1086. In 1301 Edward I arrived as a guest, and it was here that he declared his son to be the first Prince of Wales. The palace was badly damaged during the 1536 Louth Uprising against Henry VIII, but remained in use until 1586.*

Date walk completed:

# SOUTH ORMSBY, TETFORD AND TENNYSON COUNTRY

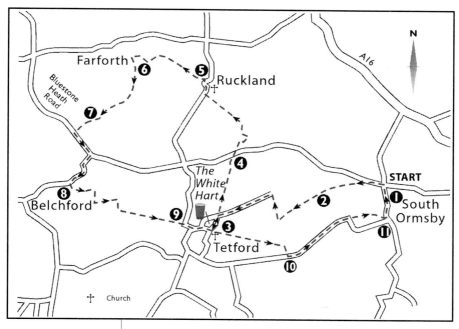

**Distance:**
12 miles

**Starting point:**
The Massingberd Arms in South Ormsby.
GR 370757

Maps: OS Landranger 122 (Skegness) or Explorer 273 (Lincolnshire Wolds South)

**How to get there:** To find South Ormsby, head south from Louth on the A16 for 7 miles, and turn right when you see a sign for Ketsby. A mile along here you cross Bluestone Heath Road. Immediately on your left you will see the Massingberd Arms, with parking spaces by the fence on the opposite side of the road.

THE PATH LEADING TO ST OLAVE'S CHURCH, BUCKLAND

*A* full day is required for this pilgrimage, for it is an adventure indeed. The steeply wooded hillsides of the Wolds are ascended several times to reveal exhilarating views before you return to the streams in the valleys below. The walk is a figure of eight, with Tetford, visited twice, at its node. It begins at an inn named after the local Massingberd dynasty and features a halt at a very special country pub. The western section of the route is a circuit of four hamlets, each with its own tiny church, and in Tetford itself you are introduced to the Grand Champion of All England and a celebrated Poet Laureate.

Though newly painted, there is no disguising the ancient origins of the **White Hart** in Tetford, looking every inch the traditional English country inn behind its tiny, lawned frontage. Step inside, and quarry-tiled floors, pine doors, and low-beamed ceilings confirm its 16th century origins. Three old stone steps lead up into the bar, where, once comfortable on the oak settle next to the open log fire, you may be reluctant to leave. There is also a small, attractive restaurant with a bay alcove overlooking the road. Meals can be eaten in either room and are chosen from the menu or snack menu, or from the specials displayed on the wall. The emphasis is on local produce, such as the Tetford sausages. It is advisable to book ahead if you are planning a Sunday lunchtime visit, when, of course, delicious roast dinners are also available. There is sticky toffee pudding for those who still have the room, and an excellent choice of real ales at the bar: Adnams, Abbot's Ale, and Fuller's London Pride among the best. Walker friendly, child friendly, and providing guest accommodation if required, you are assured of the warmest welcome at all times at the White Hart.

The White Hart serves food between 12 noon and 2 pm and between 7 pm and 9 pm, but often remains closed on Monday lunchtimes out of season.

**Telephone:** *01507 533255*
*The Massingberd Arms at the start and end of the walk is the only other source of refreshment on the route.*

 *The Walk*

① Opposite the **Massingberd Arms**, an iron kissing-gate takes you straight into the grassy parkland of **Ormsby Hall**, dominated by huge oak and beech trees, but still offering glimpses of the hall and the lake to your left. A series of white arrows marks your way to the far boundary of the park and over a stile into arable farmland, where a narrow footpath can be seen running to the left of a hedge. This path switches to the other side of the hedge before arriving at a junction of farm tracks.

② Contrary to the OS map, your route now continues straight ahead, crossing a brook and passing the edge of **Moor Holt**; just past here, it turns right to join another bridleway – this diversion is well signed throughout. Rejoining the marked route at the stables of **Fen Farm**, turn left onto **Clay Lane**, a sturdier surface, which now guides you towards **Tetford**. At a cottage on the right named **Lane End**, turn left into the lane winding towards the village church; from here the **White Hart** is just yards in front of you.

*Tetford is the largest village in the Tennyson valley, where the Poet Laureate attended meetings of the Tetford Club, a group of local gentry which met every month on the Thursday nearest to the full moon. Samuel Johnson also addressed the club in 1764 – probably from the old oak settle in the bar of the White Hart.*

*A branch of the illustrious Dymoke family lived at the Mansion House in the village, and several monuments to members of the family can be found in St Mary's church. The Dymokes have held the curious hereditary title of the Champion of the King (or Queen) for 600 years, traditionally riding into each coronation feast in full armour and challenging anyone denying the monarch's right to succeed. The wall tablet commemorating Captain Edward Dymoke is surmounted by original pieces of armour.*

③ From the church, locate a footpath between houses named **Holly Haven** and the **Maltings**, and walk along it past a white cottage, behind a garage, and over a

wooden footbridge into a meadow. Head half-right across the meadow.

A wooden footbridge over the remains of an ornamental canal guides you towards a stile and back onto the road. Here head left to **Lane End Cottage** once more, but this time continue into the cottage garden, climb over two stiles, and cross the pasture in front of you. Take several deep breaths before you negotiate the next field, where a broad clear path struggles up the longest steepest hill in the whole of the county – or so it seems. Fortunately your frequent halts will give you chance to admire the prospect of **Tetford** and surrounding fields in the valley below. Beyond a row of tall beech trees, the path carries on to a farm track. Turn left for a few yards, and then branch right again onto another diagonal field path, enjoying a fine view into a deep combe on the right before reaching the exposed **Bluestone Heath Road**.

*For 14 miles the Bluestone Heath Road maintains the highest ground possible as it traverses the Wolds. Dating back to prehistoric times, this track would have offered better progress than through the densely wooded hillsides below or the poorly drained clay valley bottoms. The wide sweeping views are breathtaking, but in bad weather the route is extremely exposed,*

**A VIEW OVER THE WOLDS FROM TETFORD**

**and nowhere along the way have any settlements ever sprung up.**

④ Now look to your right to spot a footpath sign on the opposite side of the road, at which point two stiles take you into another field and towards the farmstead of **Worlaby** – not to be confused with the village of the same name in the very north of the county. You will spot the tiniest of churches, now used as one of the estate offices. Follow the tarmac track right around the back of the farm, and then bear right to follow the fence all the way down the hillside, past a group of farm cottages, and into an area of newly established lakes. At the end of this enchanting track, an extremely steep road is reached, which should be followed to the right, down to the stream, and partway up the far bank.

⑤ In the hamlet of **Ruckland**, along the lane to your right, can be found the little church of **St Olave**, while to the left your footpath climbs a short flight of steps and skirts the edge of a field past the rectory and above a long narrow wood. On reaching a more obvious track, bear to the right, away from the stream and towards another hillside wood. Be sure to keep looking behind you – this glorious scene of grassy hills and valleys, woods, and winding streams extends in all directions. Eventually the track climbs to

another farmstead, **Farforth**, and another exquisitely maintained church.

⑥ At the church, turn right onto the surfaced lane, left along a signed bridleway, and left again onto the grassy bridleway tumbling down the hillside. Follow this track for an enjoyable mile until, at the end of a short wooded rise, you emerge in **Oxcombe**, the last of this circuit's four hamlets.

⑦ Having walked past the grand **Manor House**, you come across an intriguing octagonal turret at the corner of a walled garden. Look back here to view the more elegant turrets of the manor's Tudoresque façade before continuing along the sharply ascending lane as far as the end of the wood on your left. Here two consecutive stiles enable you to cut the corner and find yourself once more on **Bluestone Heath Road**. Peering into the dramatic 'ox combe', walk left to the signed turning for **Belchford** and descend steeply down this side road.

⑧ In half a mile, turn left at a bridleway signed for **Tetford**; then turn left again almost immediately to begin another zigzag cross field trek along a well indicated bridleway. Beyond a white-railed bridge, the route upgrades to a good chalk track, leading you all the way back into Tetford, your every step surveyed by the stark silhouette of a derelict farm on the hilltop.

⑨ In Tetford's **North Road**, the church is once again ahead of you, with the **White Hart** to its right. To continue, walk into the churchyard and round the back of the church. Clear the stile at the end of the cemetery to find yourself in open pasture; then simply plot a course straight ahead. This is the course of the Roman road to **Burgh-le-Marsh**, at that time a ferry port linking Lincolnshire with Norfolk across the Wash. Soon a stile gives reassurance that you are still on the right track, and your route maintains the same direction along a series of field paths, negotiating numerous stiles, footbridges, and kissing-gates. Eventually a clear signpost directs you to the right, along the side of a ditch, and over one last footbridge onto a road.

⑩ Now turn left along this road until, at a sharp right hand bend three quarters of a mile later, a sign directs you into the **Ormsby** parkland again. Look carefully to locate a gap in a series of fences guarding an avenue of trees which leads down to the hall. Beyond this

you pass more examples of unusual tree species as you head towards the church. Enter the churchyard through an extremely tight kissing-gate. An inspection of **St Leonard's church**, the most notable of the day, is recommended. (All of the churches visited pride themselves on their welcome, and are open on a daily basis.)

*Ormsby Hall was erected in 1752; it was the seat of a branch of the Massingberd family from Gunby Hall a few miles away. You will find monuments to the Massingberds in the church at South Ormsby, where John Wesley's father was rector in the late 1600s.*

⑪ Leave the churchyard by the main entrance, and, noting the picturesque low thatch of **Bishop's Cottage** standing in isolation in the field opposite you, turn to the left. Past a handful of estate cottages built to the same round-arch design as the **Massingberd Arms**, walk along the perimeter rail of the park to the kissing-gate and the pub at which your walk began.

Date walk completed:

# A JAUNT AROUND THE LINCOLNSHIRE WOLDS

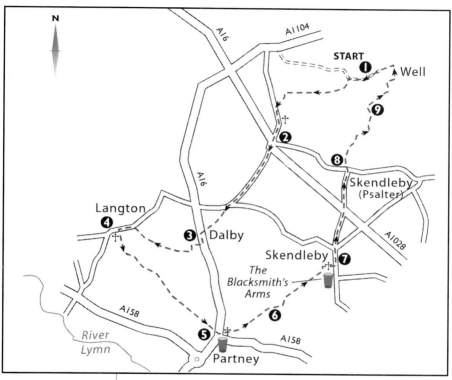

**Distance:**
10¹/₂ miles

**Starting point:**
Well.
GR 442737

Maps: OS Landranger 122 (Skegness) or Explorer 274
(Skegness, Alford, and Spilsby)

**How to get there:** *The A1104 links Alford with the A16 at Ulceby crossroads. Midway along here, a lane heads south and in less than a mile turns left towards Well village. This bend is a good place to park, where the route enters the surrounding woodlands.*

THE BLACKSMITH'S ARMS, SKENDLEBY

*O*f all that the Lincolnshire countryside has to offer, not much is missing from this expedition. Deep woodlands alternate with exposed hilly summits. You will cross from one side of the Lincolnshire Wolds to the other and then back again, and wide panoramas abound from their heights. Two of the county's finest little churches and a number of sleepy villages are discovered along the route, and the day's finale is the most arresting view across a lake to a stately mansion. Attention is required for successful navigation of the route, and some sections are muddy underfoot at certain times of year.

It goes without saying that the small ochre-brick pub that is the **Blacksmith's Arms** was once the village forge. Through the gabled porch of this unassuming façade is the most delightful and traditional little bar, where locals gather round on settles and pews by the fireplace, and a warm welcoming atmosphere is generated. To the rear of the bar is a dining room, low and cosy, with beams everywhere and an array of anvils and other memorabilia of the blacksmith's trade. This restaurant stands on the site of the deep spring-fed well of the smithy, and this has been incorporated into the newer building. (You will be invited to make a wish, of course.) The meals here have a long-standing reputation – portions are large and the quality is high. The menu is fairly traditional, but there is a specials board that changes regularly. Here the steaks – of 'finest Lincolnshire steer beef' – are a speciality, and the mixed grill is renowned. The roast lamb Henry is also popular, but a range of less substantial meals and freshly baked organic baguettes is available, and vegetarians are well catered for. On Sundays the menu is replaced by a choice of roast lunches. Among the beers stocked are Batemans and a regularly changing guest ale.

Meals are available between 12 noon and 2 pm at lunchtimes and between 6.30 pm and 9 pm in the evenings (7 pm to 9 pm on Sundays).

**Telephone:** *01754 890662*
*The Open Gate at Ulceby and the Red Lion at Partney are the only other inns found en route, but there are many places to eat and drink in nearby Alford and Spilsby.*

 *The Walk*

① From the tiny parking area at the wooded corner, set off along the concrete track into the deep woods. The trail becomes rougher and an eerieness descends where the tall trees permit no light. When you reach the floor of **Well Vale**, ascend the rough track on the opposite side until, at the limit of the woods, you turn through a gap in the hedge and continue in more or less the same direction. The path you are now on traverses two fields before uniting with a narrow plantation of young oak and sycamore to reach a junction of farm tracks. Turn left here but, when this track bends to

the right, seek a stile ahead of you through an untidy patch of farm machinery. Head for the opposite corner of the pasture you now find yourself in, crossing a stile at the entrance to **Pond Cottage** and joining the road which takes you through the valley hamlet of **Ulceby**.

② At the main road continue ahead to pass the **Open Gate Inn** on your right before branching right onto a narrow lane signed for **Fordington**. This quiet lane descends, passing the ridges and furrows of the vanished medieval village, and then rises to a junction with a road coming in from **Skendleby**. Opposite you here is a new wooden barrier; your way is through this and obliquely across the next field, passing en route a yellow marker at the corner of another enclosure. On reaching a surfaced track, execute a left-right manoeuvre to join a lesser track with a plantation alongside. A gate and stile at the end of this track usher you into a steep grassy meadow in the opposite corner of which another gate takes you onto the main road from **Louth** to **Spilsby**.

③ Turn left and walk through **Dalby**, the smallest of settlements, to locate a public bridleway sign at a gateway on the right. At this point about-turn first and walk far enough along the driveway opposite to view bow-fronted **Dalby Hall** and its minute church, a Fowler creation of 1862. Retrace your steps to cross the road and join the bridleway. Walk straight down the first meadow to the gates, diagonally left to a

gate at the far corner of the long and narrow second meadow, and then onto a broad track through the cornfields. This delightful chalky track now guides you all the way to the road in **Langton**. Turn left here to enter this leafy village. Passing the most enchanting thatched white roundhouse and a farm on your left, continue to the unusual church.

*Langton-by-Spilsby boasts one of the country's most exquisite 18th century churches. It is built on a knoll in warm red brick and capped by an octagonal bell turret. The interior resembles a college chapel and contains only the finest woodwork. A noble three-decker pulpit overlooks stepped box pews, and the altar wall is adorned by fluted oak panelling. Betjeman even acclaimed Langton as 'one of the most attractive and interesting churches in Lincolnshire – and therefore in England because Lincolnshire is rich in remarkable churches'. The church was erected by George Langton, whose grandson Bennet was held in such high esteem by his friend Dr Samuel Johnson, that he said of him 'I know not who will go to heaven if he does not.'*

THE THATCHED WHITE ROUNDHOUSE

④ Return to the farmyard you passed on your way to the church, and cross a stile on the far fence to join another long track past woods and open fields; every step along here is a delight. When this track bends sharply to the left, abandon it and keep straight ahead along a clearly visible path through two long arable fields. Circumnavigate the edge of a small copse and then continue in your former direction by keeping to the hedgerow that passes a lone yew tree. Now a better track opens up ahead of you, along which you stride for half a mile into the next village, **Partney**, with the church tower and its galleon weathervane as your target.

⑤ Go over the road and cross the churchyard into **Chapel Lane**. Head left to **Maddison's Lane**, into which you turn right. Now look for the signed footpath on the left, walk round the back of the small school, and follow the rather vague path across the next pasture, aiming to unite with the clear stream coming in from the left. This little stream, lined with tall trees and hawthorn, is your companion for the next half-mile, until a stile at the top of the fourth and longest meadow diverts you away from the water and into a higher field.

⑥ Here the pathway slants left through the crop towards a gap in the hedge ahead, and then continues unerringly in the same direction towards **Skendleby church**, now prominent on the hillside ahead. Beyond a pair of white gates, a clearer track curves through a field of cows before leaving via an unexpected footbridge on the right. A few yards along the next field-edge, the path disappears into the woods on the right before emerging into sunlight again in the churchyard high above. Before you is the huge tower of the church, and, a few yards along the road beyond this, the **Blacksmith's Arms** is on the right.

*Skendleby claims to be one of Lincolnshire's most attractive villages, and with its gabled manor, a cedar-shaded church tower, and thatched houses along the main street this cannot be disputed. Like many other villages, Skendleby is much shrunken since medieval times, and a deep linear trough – or holloway – in the field behind the inn may have been an important village street. Less than a mile from here, the Giant's Hill long barrow was excavated in 1933 and has since been carbon dated to 3500 BC. Here, beneath the elongated earthen mounds, lie a pair of Neolithic multiple burial chambers.*

⑦ Turn left out of the inn porchway and walk through the straggling village of **Skendleby**, soon arriving at a junction. Opt for the middle of the three roads in front of you (signed **Ulceby**) and climb steeply to the main road, a route once used by the Romans. Cross here, entering the unsigned lane opposite, and descend towards the red pantile roofs in the hidden spot known as **Skendleby Psalter**.

⑧ Again cross the road before you, and continue ahead, this time on a twisting grassy path which skirts the cottages before ascending sharply towards **Fordington Wood**. (What a privilege to pass through this landscape, combining woodlands and hedgerows with wide open fields and views as far as **Skegness** on the east coast. But the best is still to come.) Adhere to the path when it veers left into the wood, and branch left again immediately. This enchanting woodland roller-coaster now transports you back towards **Well**, and you need only to ensure that you turn right at the only junction and follow the very edge of the wood around **Badger Hill**.

⑨ Go along a brief open stretch and through a gate; bear left to descend sharply towards **Well Vale**, passing on your left the quite exquisite little Palladian church. Returning to the valley floor, pass to the left of the lake – from here the views of **Well Vale Hall** are stunning, a suitable reward for your day's strenuous efforts. When you reach the corner of the wood at two enormous beech trees, turn left to ascend to the road and leave this wonderful parkland. Your parking spot is now just a short walk to your left.

*Well Vale Hall was built by James Bateman in 1725, and the park and valley were landscaped at about the same time. At the corner of the lake is the chalk spring which gives the estate its name and which keeps the lake so clean. The church has four stone Tuscan columns supporting the heavy pediment, which is crowned by a later bell cupola. Its isolated position was carefully chosen in order to enhance the view from the hall.*

*Date walk completed:*

# WOODS, WATERWAYS, MILLS AND A FORGOTTEN RAILWAY

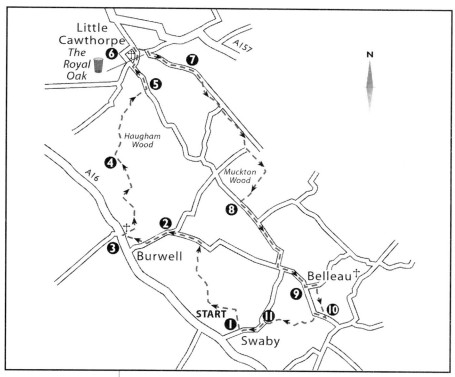

**Distance:**
11½ miles

**Starting point:**
Pinfold Lane,
Swaby.
GR 383774

Maps: OS Landranger 122 (Skegness), or Explorer 283
(Louth and Mablethorpe) and 273 (Lincolnshire Wolds South)

**How to get there:** *On the A16, 7 miles south of Louth,
turn left at the first road signed for Swaby. This is Pinfold
Lane; just half a mile along here, you should park carefully
on the grass where you see a rough-hewn bench by the
gravel bridleway on the left, signed 'Walmsgate'.*

THE DOVECOTE AT BELLEAU

*S*prings and streams are the recurring theme of this exciting expedition, where crystal-clear waters bubble up from the chalky slopes of the wolds to descend towards the coastal plain and the east coast. Entirely rural, your walk on winding lanes and magical pathways links a chain of enchanting woods and glades. You will wander through charmingly unspoilt villages, and in one of them you will find refreshment at a country inn of excellent repute.

Most people from the Louth region of Lincolnshire will be aware that Little Cawthorpe's **Royal Oak** is known locally as The Splash, thanks to its exquisite setting across a forded stream, screened by the dense trees on the opposite bank, and many will have lazed on its lawns or sought shade underneath the wide parasols. Inside, the lounge is a wonderful jumble of small rooms, dark and low, with open fires and wood panelling. A major extension to the inn has recently been completed, which comprises a spacious and elegant restaurant, several other intimate dining 'nooks', and six guest rooms above.

The food here is all of a very high quality, and local suppliers are used where possible. Most of the items on the menu are traditional dishes – Lincolnshire sausage and Grimsby haddock are favourites – but more exotic choices include chicken korma and Thai red vegetable curry, one of two vegetarian options. There is also a good selection of light snacks, while the tempting desserts may include home-made treacle sponge. On Sunday lunchtimes a roast carvery replaces the menus; as this is very popular, booking ahead is advisable. At the bar two Greene King ales are available (Abbot's Ale and IPA) as well as a guest beer such as Dixon's Major, which is brewed at Wainfleet by the former head brewer from Bateman's.

As well as normal opening hours The Splash remains open throughout the afternoon on Fridays, Saturdays, and Sundays. Meals are available between 12 noon and 2.30 pm and again from 7 pm to 9.30 pm. On Sundays meal times are 12 noon to 4 pm and 5 pm to 9 pm, but may differ out of season; please ring to confirm.

**Telephone:** *01507 600750*
*The only other place where food and drink are available en route is the Stag's Head in Burwell.*

 *The Walk*

① A fine metalled bridleway (signed to **Walmsgate**) heads north from **Pinfold Lane** and soon arrives at **High Barn**, a cluster of brick farm buildings, through which you follow the main track to the left and continue uphill on a somewhat stonier surface. Beyond the next group of barns, keep to the right of the hedge and, two long fields later, turn right onto **Cowdyke Lane**, a substantial green lane, typical of Lincolnshire, with wide grassy verges flanked by trees and hedgerows on each side. **Cowdyke Lane** eventually plunges through woods to a road below; turn left here, and begin to take in the delights along this lane: a plantation of towering ivy-clad trees, ornamental ponds linked by weirs and a crystal-clear stream, and then a curious tumbledown corner house overlooking a neglected walled garden.

② At the junction turn left towards **Burwell**, with the stream now on your left and a stark copse of fir trees on the horizon to the right. Past **Brook Farm** and more ponds, look for a signed footpath on your right; follow this over the field behind two large barns (the way is clear, even in crop). From this

95

elevated position, an excellent view over the rooftops of **Burwell** unfolds, towards which you now descend, making sure you turn left before the church to enter the village along a wide grassy bank between the houses.

*A cluster of interesting buildings around the grassy banks of the brook makes a short exploration of Burwell worthwhile. Next to the attractive Stag's Head pub, the octagonal butter cross dates back to 1690 and has served as a market hall, church hall, dovecote and village hall. Burwell was, in fact, a significant market town from the 1200s. Nearby, wrought iron gates lead you up to St Michael's church, redundant since 1981; its Norman chancel arch and monuments to the Listers from Burwell Hall were shamefully destroyed in 1958.*

③ Now head back along the path by which you entered **Burwell**, but

THE ROYAL OAK AT LITTLE CAWTHORPE

this time, rather than veering right towards the barns, follow the footpath straight up the hill until you reach a firm track. Turn left onto this and left again almost immediately, and then follow the track as indicated by the waymarker posts (in disagreement with the Ordnance Survey), turning right at the only junction, and eventually arriving at the track's end, in the middle of an arable field. From here another clear path is signed to the left through the crop in the next two fields, bringing you to the edge of an arm of **Haugham Wood**. The spire you will have spotted to the north-west is that of **Haugham**, a village church built in the 19th century as a smaller version of **Louth**.

④ Beyond the trees, the footpath crosses one more field, two stiles, and a steep valley before joining a shaded grassy track around the perimeter of this large deciduous wood. Half a mile further on, the track circles the wood's northern corner. Locate a yellow arrow indicating a path shooting across the field at right-angles, in the direction of a lone oak beside a winding chalk track. At the oak, walk left along the track for a few yards before a single plank footbridge on the right leads you onto a straight grass track, soon to emerge on the road above **Little Cawthorpe**.

⑤ Although there are field paths

which bypass the roads of **Little Cawthorpe**, the village itself is too delightful to miss. On arriving at the glade in the village centre, take the road to your right, passing a willow-shaded duckpond fed by springs and brooks cascading through the trees in the hollow. This lane wends its way past interesting cottages and houses, and soon reaches the entrance to the **Royal Oak** on your right, with the ford ahead of you.

*Seven springs feed Little Cawthorpe's shaded little village pond, and so the Long Eau river begins its journey to the North Sea. High above the springs, the black and red banded walls and wooden bell turret of St Helens' church survey the scene. The charming Victorian church is 200 years more recent than the mellow brick manor house opposite, with its Dutch gables and diamond shaped chimneys dating from 1670. Far older still are the earthworks in the fields adjacent to the river; these are the remains of Legbourne Priory, built in the 12th century for Cistercian nuns.*

⑥ From the pub driveway, go down to the ford and over the footbridge. The next section is a spot to linger after your lunch. The path alongside the clear bubbling waters of the **Long Eau** is shaded by trees on both banks; the earthworks of

Legbourne Priory are just discernible through the greenery on your left. Another, railed footbridge then leads you back onto tarmac, and you turn right at the green island into **Wood Lane**, a public bridleway taking you as far as the trackbed of the former railway linking Louth with London.

⑦ Do not stray onto the actual rail route – it holds untold horrors underfoot – but cross and continue along the extension of **Wood Lane**, itself a sometimes muddy track here. The wooded surroundings, however, are inspirational as you enter **Blindwell's Holt** and then recross the railway before leaving the wood on the indicated farm track at the white bar-gate. Progress along this track, its surface deeply rutted by heavy farm vehicles, until it makes an obvious swing to the right. At this point your route continues straight ahead, on a lesser track, to pass another holt on your right before emerging from the trees onto a wider track perpendicular to your own. Turn up the hill to the right, past a line of ancient oak trees, and enter the southern edge of **Muckton Wood**. Passing a fenced enclosure of pheasant traps, the path opens up surprisingly and rises to a hillcrest road beneath a dramatic forked beech; turn left here.

⑧ Now follows a stint of elevated road-walking. Progress is swift and the views are stupendous.

*Beyond the silver silos of Station Farm in Authorpe, the distant coastal panorama extends from Mablethorpe to Skegness, with the distinctive outlines of the snaking roller-coasters at Ingoldmells and Butlin's huge white pavilion visible.*

⑨ After 1¹/₂ miles, spotting a cream-painted cottage named **South View** on your left, turn into the side road and descend to the little village of **Belleau**. Halfway down the hillside, opposite **St Vincent's church**, locate a stile beyond which a footpath proceeds through a pasture overlooking an octagonal dovecote. This watery meadow, full of springs, ponds, and streams, is quite enchanting, but it is important to leave via the second of two high stiles on the hillside to your right; otherwise you will find yourself trapped by the electric fence. This fence overlooking the sloping meadow guides you to a public footpath sign at the opposite end of the field. Follow the short footpath down into the wood, over two footbridges, and down the track alongside a trout farm to find yourself on the roadside at **Belleau Bridge**.

⑩ Follow the road to the right for 200 yards, and then, where the road bends to the right, branch left onto a stony bridleway. Against a backdrop of tall trees, the track sweeps around the field edge in a wide arc before descending into a wood as a narrower path. This delightful stretch twists and turns along the valley of the accompanying brooklet, until, having passed through two gates, the tight valley opens up into a wooded basin at a large pond guarded by a decoy heron. You realize that your path has become a neatly trimmed lawn; instead of approaching the lakeside, you take the higher path passing directly beneath the large house on your right.

⑪ You now find yourself at the end of narrow **Valley Lane** in **Swaby**, which you follow to **Pado Lane** in the centre of the village, before turning to the left. At the crossroads a right–left manoeuvre is required before you ascend **Pinfold Lane**, soon arriving once more at the junction with the bridleway and your starting point.

*Date walk completed:*

# SALTFLEETBY AND A NATURE RESERVE

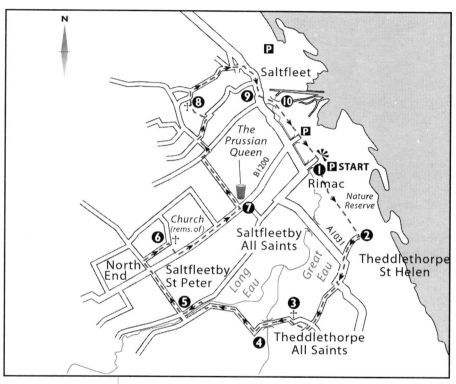

**Distance:**
11½ miles

**Starting point:**
*The car park at Rimac.
GR 468918*

Maps: OS Landranger 113 (Grimsby), or Explorer 283 (Louth and Mablethorpe)

**How to get there:** *The A1031 is Lincolnshire's coastal road, linking Grimsby with Mablethorpe. Along here, where the road turns sharply to the right 1½ miles south of Saltfleet, a lane signed 'Rimac' leads left to the car park by the sand dunes there.*

THE PUMPING STATION AT GAYTON

*H*ere is an expedition combining the two entirely different flavours of Lincolnshire's coastal marsh. The scene is set with a bracing shoreline walk through the Saltfleetby and Theddlethorpe Dunes Nature Reserve, overlooking the saltmarsh stretching to the North Sea. Turning inland, you enter a moody landscape of farmland dotted with evocative medieval churches in various stages of ruin and decay, capturing the spirit of Sir John Betjeman's *A Lincolnshire Tale*. A visit to a village inn of puzzling origin is included, and the day ends as it began, back on the sand dunes.

Why is the **Prussian Queen** so called? Most books lean towards the name of a ship wrecked upon the nearby shore – Rimac gained its name in this way – but the menu in the pub claims that the future mother of Frederick the Great sailed from Saltfleet Haven in the early 1700s. A wall plaque offers you even more preposterous options, including the tale of a royal body washed up on the beach nearby; you decide. The whitewashed building itself stands alone on this long straight road, surrounded by shrubs and a few trees. A Union Jack flies high and a riot of colourful flower baskets welcome you in. The interior, seemingly untouched for many years, has a relaxed atmosphere and friendly locals gather here. The surface of the bar itself is entirely covered with embedded pennies, and mounted on one wall is a huge ship's wheel. You might prefer the small separate dining area or even to sit outside on the large sheltered lawn to the rear. The quality of the food is excellent, and the portions generous, but the selection is limited mainly to traditional favourites. The fish pie, however, is particularly renowned, while lasagne and chilli con carne are also made to the chef's special recipes. On Sundays the three course lunches are popular, but for less hearty appetites sandwiches, jacket potatoes, and a range of lighter snacks are available. Not quite everything is prepared on the premises; the tasty sponge puddings, fruit pies, and cakes are provided by ladies who live in the locality. Draught bitters on offer include Black Sheep and Worthington, while Grolsch and Carling lagers are available; Guinness and Scrumpy Jack cider complete the line-up on the bar.

Usual licensing hours apply, and the bar remains open all day on Saturday. Lunchtime food is served between 12 noon and 2 pm seven days a week, and bar meals are available again from 7 pm every evening.

**Telephone:** *01507 338707*
*As well as the Prussian Queen and the two pubs in Saltfleet, the King's Head in Theddlethorpe All Saints is just off-route, and a finer picnic spot than Rimac would be difficult to find.*

 *The Walk*

① The seashore is an exhilarating part of this walk, and by starting at **Rimac** you both begin and end the day with a shoreline stroll. The area around Rimac itself, developed as a nature conservation area, warrants a thorough investigation before you head off to the beach and turn to the south. Of several alternative footpaths along the beach, the shore side of the dunes allows easiest progress; turn right to join your path just past a small viewing platform. Even when the tide is out, you can hear the distant roar of the crashing waves across the vast stretches of sand, littered with driftwood (including some fairly large timbers) and displaying a variety of thriving shrubs and plants. When the pathway expires, continue along the sand for half a mile until you spot a white flagpole above the dunes.

② Here a sandy path leads to another parking area, beyond which a narrow lane heads past **Kennie's**

**Farm** to the **A1031**. Join the main road for a short distance, turning right into **Station Road** at a left-hand bend (signed **Carlton**) and following this into the small village of **Theddlethorpe All Saints**. Go straight over the crossroads into **Grove Road**, and cross the footbridge on your right, leading you over a cornfield to the quite majestic church of All Saints, once the cathedral of the Marsh, but now redundant. If you find the church unlocked, the wood carving and other remaining treasures inside make a visit well worthwhile.

③ Facing the church continue left along the road for a mile until, having crossed the **Great Eau**, you come to the next feature of interest: the old pumping station at **Gayton Engine**.

*In 1850 the Gayton engine was constructed to pump water from the low marshland dykes into the Great Eau, which is higher. After conversion from steam to diesel in 1940, the engine was abandoned a decade later. In 1993 the neat white building was restored and the machinery put back into its original working order by the man who had operated it half a century earlier! On certain summer days volunteers still run the engine for the public. Two ancient preserved oak trunks, excavated from the nearby marsh, lie on the green nearby.*

④ Along the same road the **Long Eau** comes alongside, and in a further quarter of a mile you spot a single plank bridging a ditch on your right. Beyond this, a more substantial bridge crosses the **Long Eau** itself, and you find yourself on a lane facing **Manor Farm**. Turn left here and continue with the **Long Eau** now on your left.

⑤ At the crossroads turn right into **Three Bridge Lane**, which takes you to **Wain's Bridge** at the junction with the main road, where stands the newer church in **Saltfleetby St Peter**. Continue ahead into **North End Lane** and turn right into **Charles Gate** in a few hundred yards; from here you can survey the folly on your right, restored, and capped by a white observation tower. Along this lane you soon come to the abandoned medieval tower of the original church, isolated and overgrown in its eerie graveyard of ivy-covered headstones.

⑥ Walk straight through the graveyard, and on the far side join a track coming in from the left, soon to turn right along a narrow field-edge path with a ditch to its right. Go through a kissing-gate, around the right-hand perimeter of a lawned garden, and along a short driveway, to find yourself back on the main road. Turn to the left, and make your way through the long straggling village of **Saltfleetby** (meaning 'settlement by the salt stream'), which is actually three villages in one, and once boasted six churches. The silhouette of one of them looms to your right: the precariously leaning tower of **All Saints' church**. A mile along this medieval salt trade route, you at last espy an inn ahead of you – the **Prussian Queen**.

⑦ Retracing your steps from the **Prussian Queen**, turn right when the road sign directs you towards **Skidbrooke**. This long straight lane performs a zigzag at **Queen's Bridge** and advances to a crossroads at a red telephone box; turn right here into **Tilley Gate**. Just past **White House Farm** on the right, look for a public footpath sign on your left. Over a narrow footbridge, you now pursue a vague path along the left-hand edge of a series of pastures linked by footbridges and stiles, until you reach an apparent impasse in the corner of the third field. (Well, you enrolled for adventure and here it is!) The footbridge over the ditch in front of you is hidden deep in the tall dense reeds. Believe me, the bridge does exist, and faith and perseverance will see you safely onto the other side. The path continues along the left-hand edge of an arable field to

the desolate hulk of **Skidbrooke's abandoned church**, reached by a narrow rickety bridge below a sycamore.

*The people of bustling Saltfleet once had to trudge a mile across the fields to worship at the large 14th century church in Skidbrooke, now totally isolated, and redundant since 1973. If you venture inside, you may be as startled as the flapping pigeons you disturb, but the eerie mossy shell still contains an array of ancient carvings, mosaic, and window tracery.*

⑧ Go back over the footbridge and onto the footpath to arrive soon at the road linking **Skidbrooke** with **Saltfleet**. Turn to the right, and walk for almost a mile along here, with just a concrete bank between you and the wide **South Dyke** for much of the way. When you reach the main coastal road at **Saltfleet**, turn right into the village, where there is much to see.

*On the left, a pump mounted on a carved stone memorial to Frederick Freshney, a local Boer War hero, is succeeded by the huge New Inn, raised in brick in the 17th century and standing beside a group of lofty beeches.*
*The village of Saltfleet has been most things: a salt production centre, a fishing port, a market*

*town, and a fashionable bathing resort, but nowadays only seals and tourists seeking peace and quiet visit. The village's quietest and saddest spot is the beautifully restored garden of the Methodist chapel, dedicated to Saltfleet's victims of the 1953 tidal flood, many of them elderly people trapped in their own homes.*

⑨ Past a converted windmill, look out for a row of five neat coastguard cottages on the right, and after the road swings right, having crossed one creek, turn left onto a track (signed **Paradise**) to cross another, and then a third creek, beyond which your track expires at a parking area.

⑩ But your way through the grasses to the left of the dunes is clear, and you familiarize yourself once more with the sandy surroundings: to your left are the vast salt marshes; to your right the gorse, hawthorn, and sea buckthorn whose berries feed redwing, fieldfare, and other migrant birds; and a mile in front of you the gap in the dunes at Rimac through which you first emerged onto this invigorating shoreline.

*The sand dunes between Saltfleetby and Theddlethorpe form a nature reserve of national importance. The combined behaviour of the North Sea tides and stormy winds led to the formation of the dunes 600 years ago, and the geography of the area is still undergoing constant change. Excellent information boards index a wealth of plant and wildlife too profuse to list in full here, but some species are of particular interest. The orange-berried sea buckthorn, though abundant here, is scarce elsewhere in Britain, while fancifully named viper's bugloss and fieldmouse-ear also grow here. Samphire picked from the saltmarsh is delicious cooked and eaten with vinegar, and marsh orchids can be found in the freshwater area behind the dunes. Look out for natterjack toads, and darting damselflies and dragonflies.*

Date walk completed:

# TETNEY MARSHES

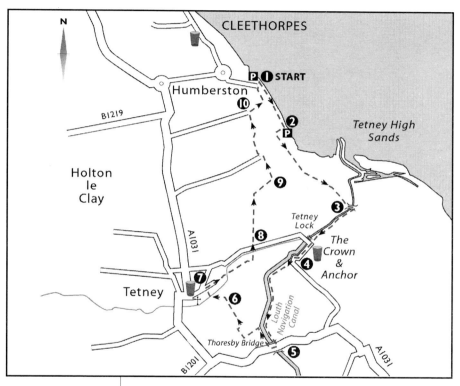

**Distance:**
9½ miles

**Starting point:**
Anthony's Bank,
Humberston.
GR 332062

Maps: OS Landranger 113 (Grimsby) or Explorer 283
(Louth and Mablethorpe)

**How to get there:** *From Cleethorpes head south-east
along the coast road (King's Road). Pass a large theme park
on your left and continue ahead to enter Thorpe Park, a
vast modern caravan site. Just before the gates into the
'Fitties', turn left onto a roughly surfaced area overlooking
the estuary; this is Anthony's Bank.*

THE CROWN & ANCHOR AT TETNEY LOCK

*H*ere's one for the ornithologists. This lengthy ramble along the raised coastal path above Tetney Marshes and the banks of the disused Louth Navigation Canal is rich in bird life, and a number of nature reserves have been established to protect the birds and their habitats. Glorious panoramas of the Humber estuary are one highlight, and a visit to a welcoming inn beside the canal is another. The canal, the sea, the Blow Wells at Tetney – water is everywhere, and you should expect the going underfoot to be muddy.

The handsome **Crown and Anchor** enjoys a prime position by the bridge crossing the Louth Navigation Canal. It is a joy to sit here surrounded by large baskets and tubs overflowing with brightly coloured flowers and survey the anglers on the bank below, their gaze focused on the canal waters. Inside the cosy bar, furnished with beams and wall timbers, most people will congregate around the fire area, locals and diners alike. You may sit in the larger dining room to the rear, if you wish, or even on the shaded private lawn behind the inn. Mainly traditional, the menu includes fresh battered North Sea haddock and excellent steaks and sauces. The lock gate chicken is served in a wine, mushroom, and tomato sauce, and the lockkeeper's mixed grill should be enough to defeat even the most ravenous rambler! Additional choices are displayed on a wallboard, and an extensive range of lighter meals is also offered – but be sure to leave some room for that ice cream from Sargent's of Hibaldstow. Alongside Bass, Caffrey's, and John Smith's Smoothflow on the bar sit Highgate Brewery Dark Mild and a changing guest beer.

The Crown and Anchor serves meals between 12 noon and 2 pm (3 pm on Sundays) and from 7 pm in the evenings. No food is served, however, on Mondays and Tuesdays.

**Telephone:** *01472 388291*

*To locate alternative refreshments on the walk you have to divert to the pub in Tetney village, although there are numerous outlets catering for the tourist trade near to Anthony's Bank.*

 *The Walk*

**The whole region covered by the walk is an ornithologist's paradise, with several bird and nature reserves passed en route. The entire seaward side of the path's coastal section forms Tetney Marshes Nature Reserve, and after meeting the gregarious swans on the old boating lake look for golden and grey plover, shelduck, and Brent geese. There is another reserve at Tetney Blow Wells and a private one alongside the track close to the Fitties. The beach and dunes between Anthony's Bank and Cleethorpes are designated a Site of Specific Scientific Interest, where dunlin, knot, and plover are among the species that feed on the teeming life in the mud, before setting off on their migratory route known as the East Atlantic highway.**

① Looking out to sea from the car park, climb the new wooden ramp to your right and proceed along the embankment, absorbing a superb view over the breakwaters on the shore to the ships plying back and forth along the **Humber Estuary**.

**Haile Sand fort is seen at close quarters, with the twin fort of Bull Sand further out to sea. Spurn lighthouse on the distant north bank is also clear.**

Continue as far as the yacht club and follow the fence over the slipway and round the corner to a parking area which slopes down to a neglected boating lake, colonized by swans and a number of species of ducks and waterfowl.

② You may see walkers on the labyrinth of paths and creeks on the other side of the lake, but any attempt to pick a route through here is doomed to frustration. Your path skirts the right-hand edge of the lake, turning left when you reach the sea embankment. This raised grassy bank leads you above the marshes for a mile and a half, with an excellent prospect over the rich arable coastal plain to your right. Note the indestructible concrete shelters known as pillboxes, defensive relics from the Second World War. Passing underneath the distinctive angular oil pipe, the path ends abruptly on the banks of the Louth Navigational Canal.

*It took five years to build the 12-mile canal between Louth Riverhead and Tetney Haven, but in 1770 the Louth Navigation Canal finally opened to sloops and sailing barges carrying grain and wool towards Grimsby and Hull, and bringing coal and timber in the opposite direction. Several of the eight locks along the canal were constructed to a unique barrel-shaped design to withstand the pressure imposed by the marshy surrounding land. Between Tetney and the sea, however, the canal was continually subject to silting up, and it was this strangulation as much as the improving rail and road network that led to the closure of the canal to freight in 1938.*

③ Take the track to the left, which soon wheels round to cross the wide canal via a huge sluice gate. Then join the opposite canal bank by clearing a stile and going through an open gate on your right. (Ornithologists may choose to branch left after

**FEEDING TIME ON THE BOATING LAKE AT HUMBERSTON 'FITTIES'**

the stile to follow the canal to **Tetney Haven**, where the sea is met and a wide range of important bird species flourishes.) Otherwise, pursue this lovely waterside pasture, cropped short by cattle, for a full mile, passing the new **Tetney lock** before going over a stile. Soon, on your left, overlooking the canal bridge and countless anglers, appears the **Crown and Anchor**.

④ From the inn, carry on along the canal bank, and opposite **Sloop House** on the left cross a stile on the right to join a signed footpath. Remain faithful to this grassy canal bank path for the next 1$\frac{1}{2}$ miles. More views unfold over the hills of the **Lincolnshire Wolds** and the incongruous but visually dramatic drums of the nearby oil terminal. The path narrows as it passes below a brick warehouse of 1821 next to **Thoresby Bridge**.

⑤ At the road, cross the canal and begin the return journey along the opposite bank, noting the original canal machinery and stonework. Soon the path angles away from the canal by adhering to the bank top around a rectangular flood-relief area built in 1970. On the third side of the oblong, descend to an obvious wooden footbridge on the left and follow the path on the other side of it. Upon meeting a farmtrack, cross with a right-left movement, and then ensure that you keep to the right of the ditch ahead of you, soon to arrive at a wood.

⑥ Turn to the right, and, keeping the wood to your left, follow its edge round to the left via a footbridge, below which the crystal-clear stream betrays the blow wells bubbling up amongst the trees nearby.

*Tetney Blow Wells are a series of deep reservoirs of artesian well water forced up through the surface clay from the chalk far below. It is the same layer of chalk which forms the hilly wolds to the west, and heavy rain on the high ground soon causes the pressure to rise in the wells at Tetney. The secluded area of the wells is densely wooded and is now a sanctuary for birds, wildlife, and plants.*

Another two fields and a footbridge further on, head diagonally right, away from the area of the wells to locate a narrow bridge in a hedgerow leading up to a more substantial footbridge over the **Tetney Drain**. Ahead of you, a stile leads you along the edge of a paddock to a kissing-gate and then along a narrow passage into the village of **Tetney**.

⑦ Unless you wish to explore the village itself, walk along the road to the right but do not follow it around the left-hand bend, opting instead for the gravel lane ahead of you (**Mill Race**). Towards the end of this lane, look carefully for a hidden stile on the left, which takes you into a paddock. Beyond a fenced footbridge, walk to the left of a tumbledown barn and across the field to a bright stile between a row of conifers and an enclosed yard opposite you. At the end of the narrow passage, cross the wide bridge and continue straight ahead onto the stony track leading into open countryside once more. In half a mile, turn onto an unsigned footpath to the left of a ditch; this takes you to a concrete footbridge directly in front of the eleven huge oil storage tanks.

⑧ Cross the main road carefully and take the metalled road to the right of the oil terminal. This is **Newton Marsh Lane**, which downgrades to a stony track as it rounds a water treatment plant before taking you between charming high hedgerows to the point where a signed footpath crosses the track.

⑨ Turn left here onto the visible path across the field, and then continue in the same direction to rejoin the track. One mile later, having passed a nature conservation area on the left and a new golf course on the other side, you arrive at the Fitties holiday park in **Humberston**.

⑩ Through the turnstile adjoining the green gates, turn right immediately onto the signed footpath through the caravan site, keeping a chain of ornamental ponds on your left. When you reach a narrow road, follow it to the left, and then take a right-hand side road at a bungalow named **Listervale**; the road ahead is marked a dead end. Now spot another signed footpath passing to the left of a house painted black and white, behind which a new wooden footbridge leads over a small stream and up onto a low straight embankment. Follow this bank to the left for just 400 yards, and there on the opposite side of the road is **Anthony's Bank**.

*Date walk completed:*

# ROTHWELL AND NETTLETON

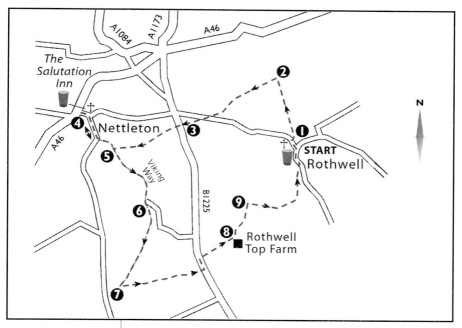

**Distance:**
9 miles

**Starting point:**
*The Blacksmith's Arms in Rothwell.
GR 151996*

**Maps: OS Landranger 113 (Grimsby) or Explorer 284 (Grimsby, Cleethorpes, and Immingham)**

**How to get there:** *At Caistor Top on the A46, high above the village of Caistor itself, is a junction of five major roads. Here select the B1225 (signed 'Horncastle'), and a mile along this road turn left into the lane signed to Rothwell. In Rothwell please park considerately on the roadside.*

'THE GREAT WALK', ROTHWELL

*D*ramatic views, unsuspected in Lincolnshire, are unveiled on this strenuous walk through the wolds at their highest. Our route takes us up one valley where nature has reclaimed the grassy slopes from the ravages of an iron mining heritage, and down another of cultivated beauty and colour, the legacy of a knighted local landowner. Sections of the Viking Way and the Neville Cole Way are included, as is an ancient high-level drover's route. There are few prettier villages from which to start an excursion than Rothwell, and a welcoming inn awaits in Nettleton, at the farthest point of the walk.

Conspicuous at the foot of the steep incline ascending the Wolds between Lincoln and Grimsby, the **Salutation Inn** in Nettleton has been an important refreshment stop for many centuries. Today locals, travellers, and ramblers gather here to create a lively, cheerful atmosphere. The interior of the pub is old and unspoilt, and the pictures on the walls together with the local chit-chat conjure up images of hunting and gamekeeping – this is, after all,

'Lincolnshire Poacher' country. The accent on game continues in the menu, with pan-fried pheasants' breasts and venison available according to season. Other dishes such as Oldham's beef (in a red wine and onion gravy), Blue Mountain fillet steak (topped with melted Stilton), and chicken forestières (with a wine and mushroom sauce) are well-established favourites here. The sandwiches, made with deep fresh crusty bread, are renowned, as are the traditional hot puddings, such as treacle tart and spotted Dick. A good selection of real ales – Tom Woods, Taylor's Landlord and Wadworth 6X among them – has led to CAMRA awards, and may lead to you finding it difficult to leave this comfortable hostel to resume your walk.

The Salutation is open during normal licensing hours, with lunchtime meals available from 12 noon to 2 pm. Evening meals start at 6 pm, but not until 7 pm on Sundays.

**Telephone:** *01472 851228*
*The Blacksmith's Arms in Rothwell at the start and end of the walk can also offer fine meals.*

 *The Walk*

① Begin by walking to the left of the **Nickerson's Arms** and turning into **Wold View**. Here, on the left, an obvious metalled bridleway now strikes steeply uphill alongside a neat hedge. Having downgraded to a farm track near the isolated farmstead of **Rothwell Stackgarth**, the track continues straight over one crossing and, half a mile further on, turns left at another, alongside a row of prickly hawthorn.

② Now follow this lovely upland track for a mile, enjoying a good view of **Pelham's Pillar** rising from an ocean of trees whose planting it commemorates. When another track bars your way, turn left onto it for a few yards and then right along a path through an arable field, as indicated by the yellow arrow. Through a gap in the hedge ahead, cross the road to enter the farm driveway, and continue in your original direction by turning immediately right onto a signed bridleway sheltered by yet another high hedge. Soon you arrive at the **B1225**, **Caistor High Street**, which was an ancient drove road to Horncastle.

③ Cross the road and on the other side maintain your progress along the track, here forming part of the **Neville Cole Way**. Do not turn left with this track, but continue straight ahead on a more deeply rutted track plunging down the hillside.

*Spreading out below you, the views over the valley towards Nettleton are stupendous. Beyond lies the vast plain of the Ancholme Valley, and further still power stations on the other side of the distant Trent can be seen, while the eagle-eyed may spot the Humber Bridge and even Lincoln Cathedral.*

Past a picturesque group of tumbledown farm buildings on your left, you soon arrive at an oak stile which was erected as a memorial to Neville Cole and bears the inscription 'The fields his study, Nature was his book'. Now keep to the muddy track past the farm and along the lane into **Nettleton**, turning right at a junction by a cluster of white cottages. In half a mile, having passed the elevated and exposed church on your right, you arrive at the **Salutation Inn**.

*The weathered tower of St John the Baptist's church in Nettleton was built from local ironstone in Anglo-Saxon times, and glows a rich ruddy brown colour in sunshine. The main body of the church, rebuilt by Fowler in 1870, is spacious and exuberant.*

④ From the **Salutation Inn** strike out once more along **Church Street** and retrace your steps as far as the **Neville Cole stile**, once more

THE SALUTATION INN, NETTLETON

accompanied by the thrilling Wolds scenery.

⑤ Now step onto the grass to the right of the stile and follow the course of **Nettleton Beck** up the valley, making sure to keep a large pond to your right. Even when the beck is out of view, the gurgling waters can still be heard. By a wooden footbridge a huge natural bowl opens up on the left, with the trees of **Tugdale Wood** crowning a central promontory high above the steep grassy slopes. Souvenir photograph hunters will find no better spot than this. Past another, smaller amphitheatre, a stile takes you onto a steep farm track. Detour to the right, if you wish to view a small hidden lake. Otherwise, ascend to the left to follow the clear diversion signs onto a woodland track on the right. Pass two arched brick mining adits, now blocked, on your left before descending to a third adit near to two more stiles. At this point look behind you to inspect a tunnel, which until recently was part of this public right of way, but is now in too dangerous a state of decay to allow passage.

*It is hard to imagine that between 1929 and 1969 this tranquil valley was ravaged by mining operations as ponies, trucks, and an underground railway removed vast quantities of Claxby ironstone from these hillsides. The ore was then loaded onto an aerial ropeway for transport to the railway at Holton le Moor. At their peak, the mines employed almost 200 people, but the iron ore was of low quality, and in 1969 the steelworks at Scunthorpe switched to cheaper Swedish ore.*

⑥ The stiles take you out of the wood and back towards the beck, with the hills now closing in more steeply. Here, as the sheep and rabbits scurry away, you embark upon a more marked ascent.

*Three further indentations on your left indicate a series of glacial dry valleys, although the going underfoot may make this seem a misleading term. Also above you to the left, spot a group of rocks where an outcrop appears to have broken through the clay surface. A closer inspection, however, reveals that this is not the chalk of which these hills are made but a stack of ironstone blocks, presumably (if inexplicably) debris from the mining industry downstream.*

At a pronounced kink in the fence, clear water bubbling from a spring tells you that you have reached the source of **Nettleton Beck**, and from here onwards the valley is dry. Cross over a final stile to follow a line of telegraph poles to the head of the valley; then turn sharp left to follow the line of the hedge.

⑦ You are immediately king of all you survey, with a sensational view of the whole of the valley you have just ascended to your left. On the horizon to the right rises a nearby radar tower, its permanently spinning dish recently replaced by a huge white sphere – a gigantic golf ball on top of a gigantic tee! A good mile along this path, you again meet **Caistor High Street**, which you follow carefully to the left for 200 yards. Then turn right onto a track when you reach the red barns of **Nettleton Bottom Farm**.

⑧ At the group of brick buildings comprising **Rothwell Top Farm**, the track swings to the left and descends towards a beech plantation. You will have noticed that these neat cultivated surroundings are in stark contrast to those of the wild Nettleton Beck valley; this is the private estate of Sir Joseph Nickerson, and the track you are on is the **Great Walk**, established by him in 1951.

⑨ Adhere to the main route throughout the **Great Walk**, not allowing bridge, gate, or stile to divert you, until you reach the public road leading down into **Rothwell**, with the dazzling white façade of the **Blacksmith's Arms** now directly ahead of you.

*Rothwell is a village of great beauty, where three valleys meet and a clear brook babbles over its stony bed opposite the long low village inn. Sir Joseph Nickerson, knighted for his services to industry in 1983, based his seed empire here, and his impact on the countryside is unmistakable. His fields are lined by immaculate A-shaped hedges, and it was he who created the Great Walk. The walk is a blaze of colour in all seasons, even in winter when bright red dogwood, yellow willow, and bulrushes adorn the banks of the ponds and streams. Look out for a wayside bench hewn out of part of an outsized tree stump. The church in the village – 'a very special church' according to Henry Thorold – is well worth a detour for its Saxon tower and Norman nave arcades.*

Date walk completed:

# FOREST TRAILS AND THE RIVER TRENT AROUND SCOTTER

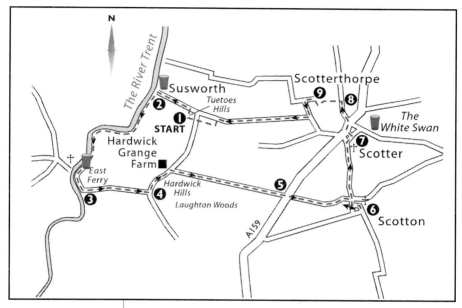

**Distance:**
11½ miles

**Starting point:**
Tuetoes Hill car park in Laughton Woods.
GR 845014

Maps: OS Landranger 112 (Scunthorpe) or Explorer 280 (Isle of Axholme)

**How to get there:** *From the centre of the village of Scotter, 6 miles south of Scunthorpe on the A159, a lane signed for Susworth heads west; 2½ miles along here, another lane (signed Laughton) heads left into Laughton Forest, and a few yards along here the Tuetoes car park is on your right.*

THE RIVER EAU IN SCOTTER

*T*his walk may be one of the most straightforward in the book, but it is as varied as any, and nowhere can woodland more enchanting than Laughton Forest be found. You are fortunate enough to pass through the forest twice, with an interlude in the form of a breezy stroll along the raised open banks of the mighty River Trent. And in a former market town – still a fascinating village – there is a warm welcome waiting for you at an inn above a small river.

The original old building of the **White Swan** in Scotter has almost been overwhelmed by later additions, but it still looks handsome enough from the grassy riverbank by the bridge over the River Eau, or from the village green further up the hill. The main lounge is a large rambling space retaining lots of original features, most noticeably huge beams across the ceiling. The lounge becomes darker and more intimate towards the panelled ingle, where a large white swan is displayed in a glass case; the best tables are here. In contrast is the enormous new dining room to the rear. Both areas always seem to be busy; this is clearly a very popular place. The menu is extensive and mouth-watering, and there are even more options on a specials board. Turner's black pudding tower is just one of the starters you might choose before moving on to the main course. Here, as well as the popular grills and home-made pies, there are Scotter's trotters (pork fillets in a sweet curry sauce) and drunken bullock (sirloin steak in a sauce flamed with whisky and barley wine). The specials might include monkfish in lemon and ginger, and there are always three vegetarian options – oh, and there's roast beef and Yorkshire pudding on Sundays, of course. Webster's and John Smith's are the usual beers, while three guest beers might include Black Sheep, Tom Woods, and Bomber County.

Usual licensing hours apply, but the inn also stays open throughout the afternoon on Fridays, Saturdays, and Sundays. Meals are served between 11.30 am and 2.30 pm, and begin again at 6.30 pm on Monday to Thursday. From Friday to Sunday meal times are from 11.30 am through to about 9 pm.

**Telephone:** *01724 762342*
*Other inns around the walk are the Jenny Wren at Susworth, the Glengarry at East Ferry, and the Three Horseshoes at Scotton.*

 *The Walk*

① Do not exit the **Tuetoes** car park by the road; instead, about-turn and head along a sandy track away from the highway. In only 100 yards – currently the line to which the fir trees have been felled – locate on your right a pathway aiming for a fenced corral. Here three successive gates take you onto the road; turn left and walk on carefully for half a mile to reach the tiny village of **Susworth**. Unless you wish to visit the **Jenny Wren Inn**, turn left just before the pub into the lane signed for **East Ferry**.

② Beyond a cultivated field on your right, the mighty **River Trent** comes alongside and you climb the raised grassy bank and follow the broad slow muddy river for a full 2 miles. Even when the road veers away, do not forsake your banktop path. Only when progress is barred by a fence should you descend and continue on the road through **East Ferry**, an unexceptional straggling settlement.

*At a war memorial at the far end of the village, the Trent bank may again be ascended for views of the jetties and boats at Owston Ferry on the far bank. This was once a town of importance, and, as well as of the ferry itself, it was the site of Roger de Mowbray's 11th century castle.*

③ Your route now leaves the river at right-angles along the quiet lane signed to **Laughton**, with **Hardwick Hill** clearly visible rising from the forest. A mile along here **Laughton Forest** is re-entered and a junction reached.

④ Turn left here and after half a mile, opposite the entrance to **Hardwick Grange Farm**, turn right onto a clear track and embark upon a stretch of magical woodland walking, the way ahead arrow-straight and every step a joy.

*The pine-clad slopes of Hardwick Hill were once the site of Roman metal working and possibly of a military garrison guarding the Trent. In addition to iron slag from the foundry, Roman coins, pottery, and ornaments have been unearthed here.*

THE WHITE SWAN INN, SCOTTER

⑤ In two miles you emerge at **Rainford's Corner**; cross the main road carefully and continue in your original direction along the lane ahead. Even when this lane peters out, remain on course and follow the enclosed track ahead of you. Straight and broad initially, the path narrows before twisting and turning into the village of **Scotton**. (Scotton is well worth exploring; look out for a pair of curious carved stone figures set into an ivy-clad archway near the church.)

⑥ Your route, however, is in the opposite direction, and a mile of brisk walking along this road leads you past an attractive brick school dated 1931 into the bustling village of **Scotter**. Turn right into **Church Lane**, where you spot the Church Centre on the corner, and walk into the churchyard. After visiting the notable Perpendicular church, leave via the path hugging the left-hand edge of the churchyard, which guides you down the hill to the green. Fine buildings surround the green, but the one you seek – the **White Swan** – is soon spotted to your right.

*Scotter is the largest village in north Lincolnshire and was once a thriving medieval market town. Richard I granted the market charter in 1190, and 25 years later his brother, King John, stayed at the Manor House, while*

120

*his men and their commanding officer lodged at the nearby inn. In honour of their visit, the inn was renamed the Sun and Anchor, the emblem of the officer. (As a pub name still in use today it is believed to be unique.) The colossal tower of St Peter's church, which presides over the village, contains a set of ringers' rules, written in black and red Elizabethan lettering and mounted above the belfry door.*

⑦ On leaving the **White Swan**, stroll down to the green banks of the **River Eau**. There are ducks to feed at this attractive spot, but no white swan to be seen. Cross the bridge, turn left, and follow the riverside to the main road through **Scotter**, turning right onto it. In a few hundred yards, **Moor Road** branches off to the left, and half a mile along here a signed footpath takes you into the arable fields to your left.

⑧ Your way is clear, and, having crossed a new wooden footbridge, the footpath continues along the edge of the field, turning sharply to the right before a short fenced lane leads you into the tiny tree-shaded hamlet of **Scotterthorpe**.

⑨ Turn left at the paddock and walk up the lane to the only junction, at which you turn left by a high curving creeper-clad wall. Turn right at the junction with the road to **Susworth** and proceed with care. Past the old deciduous trees of **Scotter Wood** on the left, the tall dark pines of **Laughton Forest** again begin to fill the horizon. On reaching the forest and passing the first bungalow, enter once more into these beguiling woodlands. With the tall pines on your left and a plantation of silver birch to your right, look out for the first clear path leading off to the right. This simple trail now guides you back to the forest road, with the car park at **Tuetoes Hill** just in front of you.

*Colonized by humans since the Stone Age, the area of Laughton Forest was once a sandy heath of shifting dunes dotted with small woods and ponds. It was first planted between 1783 and 1789, and is now managed by the Forestry Commission, who are returning large sections to their earlier state. Many walks bisect these acres of conifers interspersed with silver birch and other deciduous trees, and you may catch sight of roe deer, squirrels, and green woodpeckers.*

*Date walk completed:*

# BURTON-UPON-STATHER AND THE CLIFF

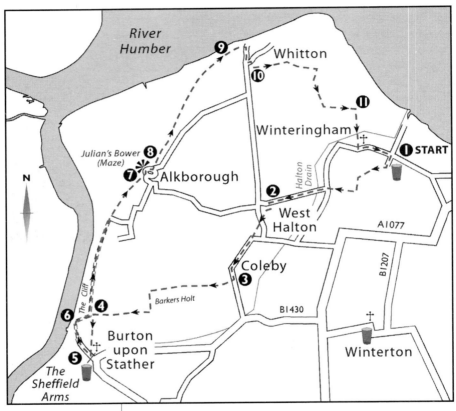

**Distance:**
12 miles

**Starting point:**
Winteringham.
GR 933222

Maps: OS Landranger 112 (Scunthorpe), or Explorer 281
(Ancholme Valley) and Explorer 291 (Goole and Gilberdyke)

**How to get there:** *Head north on the A1077 from
Scunthorpe. In 8 miles the first of three signed roads leads
off left into the village of Winteringham. All three meet at
the crossroads in the centre of the village, where you
should park considerately by the roadside.*

THE TURF MAZE AT ALKBOROUGH

*H*idden away in the county's north-westernmost corner, this area offers an exciting day's walking. Breathtaking panoramas from the top of a long high ridge encompass a large expanse of neighbouring Yorkshire and the area where three mighty rivers converge. Links with the nobility at nearby Normanby Hall and a unique maze with a mystery-shrouded history are features of this excursion along mainly rural footpaths, tough-going in sections, but thrilling throughout .

Historic indeed is the **Sheffield Arms**, its high brick gables dominating one end of Burton's High Street and the hillside falling away past the adjacent church to the Trent below. Dating back to 1664 and originally named the Black Bull, the inn was renamed in honour of the Sheffield family, resident in the area since the 16th century. The pub has a reputation for first class food in most welcoming surroundings. The meals on offer are all freshly cooked here, are locally sourced wherever possible, and cater for all tastes. A specials inset will usually include a home-made pie – beef, mushroom, and Guinness, maybe. On Sundays, however, the menu is replaced by a choice of roasts of the day, and booking is advisable.

Meals are served every day from 12 noon to 2.30 pm (3 pm on Sundays) and from 6 pm to 9 pm.

**Telephone:** *01724 721555*
*You will find other inns in East Halton and Winteringham, the Bay Horse in the latter also serving good meals.*

 # The Walk

① Strike up the hill from the **Bay Horse inn** in **Winteringham**, away from the boats in the nearby haven. At a clear junction, turn right from **High Burgage** into **Cliff Road**, and note the restored village pump on your right. Soon into open countryside, elevated and exposed, follow **Cliff Road** for about half a mile, and locate the second signed footpath on your right – be careful, the first takes you back to the church in Winteringham. The footpath descends into a shallow valley and then crosses a footbridge and the bed of a disused railway which served the numerous quarries nearby. Rather vague across the next field, the route soon improves to a farmtrack at a bridge over **Halton Drain**, and then to a tarmac surface at **Greenacres**.

② Now in the little village of **West Halton**, turn left into **Cross Street** and then right into **West Street**, maybe first visiting the **Butcher's Arms**, a striking cream and red building and a surprising find in so small a settlement. At the end of **West Street**, take the lane to the left, curve around the green, go past the sycamore-shaded church, and turn left again onto another road. At a paddock on your right, two stiles open onto a path through crop; if in place, this path provides a convenient short cut across the corner. Otherwise, go along **Coleby Road**; turn right at the major junction, and follow the road into the even smaller hamlet of **Coleby**.

③ Here, having passed between the high-walled manor, look for a public bridleway sign just past the last house on the right. This pleasant lane, firm and enclosed by tall hedgerows initially, guides you for a full mile at an almost undetectably rising gradient, and then veers sharply to the left before joining a better lane at **Barker's Holt**, a long thin band of pine trees, where you turn right. Then head unerringly west, passing a colossal water tower, and walking along a short stretch of road and into a wood ahead, identified as a picnic spot.

④ Only when you have crossed a bridge over a concrete gully should you deviate, turning left alongside the stream. This woodland path parts company with the stream but continues as a grassy corridor towards **Burton upon Stather**. Past a fire beacon and a set of railings, the way narrows and twists to emerge into the sunlight between Burton's distinguished church and a green where the Tuesday market, first granted a charter in 1315, was once held. At the steep road, climb the last few yards to your destination: the **Sheffield Arms** at the head of Burton upon Stather's **High Street**.

*Burton, as you will discover, is really two separate villages. Burton upon Stather, where the Sheffield Arms is sited, overlooks the Trent from the top of the cliff, while Burton Stather is the straggling settlement lining the river bank itself – 'stather' means staithes or wharves. There are quaysides serving shipping traffic, and a ferry once plied from here across the Trent to Garthorpe and*

*back. Along here can be seen the remains of ramps running down into the river; under the supervision of Barnes Wallis, these were used in the Second World War for testing secret waterproofed 'submarine' tanks in readiness for the Rhine crossing. The church on the cliff contains interesting monuments to the Sheffields, who built nearby Normanby Hall in 1825 and who have lived there since. The family's most illustrious member was Sir John Sheffield, who fought against the Dutch in the battle of Sole Bay in 1672 and who eventually became Duke of Buckingham and Normandy. Much of their Regency mansion – and its extensive gardens – is open to the public and is well worth a visit if time allows.*

⑤ Turn right out of the pub and stride down **Stather Road**, enjoying the first intimate views of the broad **River Trent** below you. When you reach another pub near the end of the road, the opportunity of walking right to the water's edge presents itself, though you will then have to regain all the height you have just lost.

⑥ Turning right onto a signed bridleway at the road's end, ignore a second right-hand turn into a caravan site and pursue the delightful – if steep – woodland path ahead of you. Eventually, you will recognize the bridged gully from your outward journey. Just beyond here, locate a grassy bridleway branching off to the left and steadily gaining height as it traces the edge of the clifftop.

*The views now are simply stupendous. At the foot of the precipitous bank clad in bright yellow gorse, the lazy Trent sweeps towards a huge distant bend. Focus your gaze on the horizon, where plumes of steam rise from far-off power stations. Can you see York Minster? Even* *the hills of the Peak Distict, almost 60 miles away, are visible.*

The path enters a fenced section with a dense wood on the Trent side and a row of towering beeches on the other. Alternating between enchanting woodland and the open cliff overlooking the vast valley, every step of this bridlepath is to be savoured, until it concludes abruptly in a clearing near to **Alkborough**. You have arrived at **Julian's Bower**.

*Julian's Bower is Lincolnshire's only remaining turf maze. Though records first mention the maze in*

WHITTON'S VILLAGE CHURCH

*1697, its origins are much more ancient and shrouded in mystery. Turf mazes were once common and often bore the name Julian's Bower. Maze patterns were adopted by the early church as symbols of the path to salvation, and it has been suggested that Alkborough's was first cut by monks from nearby Walcot. In Elizabethan and Stuart times, turf mazes, like hedge mazes, were mainly used for sport. A miniature version of the 44 ft diameter maze can be seen in the church, where an iron copy is cut into the stone of the porch floor, and a further representation is set in the stained glass of the east window.*

⑦ **Alkborough**, like Burton, displays a fine mix of brick and stone buildings as you stroll through the village to **St John the Baptist's church**, set behind a magnificent old conifer avenue. Walk along **Church Street** to the left of the churchyard, cross a pleasant green and a low-level track, where you will spot the arches and basins of **Low Wells springs**, and enter the field ahead of you via the gate. A new path ushering you to the right of this field appears to be planned, but at the time of writing the only option is to hug the wooden fence beyond the gate until a **Neville Cole Way** sign at a stile endorses your route-finding ability.

*James Neville Cole, MBE devoted his life to the protection and development of public rights of way in north Lincolnshire, and founded many rambling clubs here, including, in 1932, Grimsby's Wanderlust Rambling Club. The Wanderlust Way, a circular 20-mile walk on the far side of the Wolds, is one tribute to his work, and another, the Neville Cole Way, was founded by his many friends as a lasting memorial. The way is 57 miles in length and ends in Nettleton, where it meets the Viking Way.*

⑧ Now a grassy terrace and two more stiles lead you onto a road, which you cross to carry on along the inside of the field opposite. Again, the path continues along the top of the cliff through an ever-changing landscape – now a wood, now a meadow, now a field border. The only hiccup is at a curious brick ruin, which appears to serve purely as shelter for walkers; here look carefully on the right to locate a stile taking you into a wood. Another leading landmark – the mighty **Humber Bridge** – now comes into view, soon to vanish when you cross a stile on your left and continue along a sloping sheep meadow. You have not been on close terms with the Trent for some time now, and, although the river sidles back towards you, there is to be no reunion; you have passed the confluence of the **Trent** and the **Ouse**, and it is the **River Humber** which now flows below you.

⑨ The route through the pasture eventually arrives at a stile near a road in **Whitton**, the most isolated of the villages in this corner of Lincolnshire. Turn right into **Main Street**, having first admired the proud church tower capped by a pantiled pyramid. Soon turn left into **Old Mill Lane**, but, instead of following the lane to the left, look for a footpath curving between the houses on the right, leading you through to **Ings Lane**; turn left here.

⑩ This firm track will speed you along for almost a mile until, at its terminus, you swing right to follow a narrow path beside a deep channel. Cross the wooden footbridge, and continue along the field edge to the next finger post, just 30 yards away. Survey the field on your right carefully. A ditch begins near to another clear sign a few yards into the field. The sign points diagonally through the cornfield, the true direction of the right of way. But, if the path is not in place, you will prefer to accompany the ditch all the way to the track at the far end of this long field. Head left along the track – **Rotten Sykes Lane** – to its meeting with a road.

⑪ At this point, turn right onto an obvious path leading straight towards the church tower in **Winteringham**. Towards the church, a footbridge takes you to **Meggitt's Lane**, where the church can be inspected at close quarters. Past the church, follow the lane to the left and admire the fine old houses of **Winteringham** as you make your way back to the crossroads at the **Bay Horse**.

 *Date walk completed:*

128